The Ultimate T Air Fryer Cookbook for Beginners

Affordable Delicious & Effortless Tefal Air Fryer Recipes to Easy Fry, Grill, Roast and Bake

Julie B. McKeen

All Rights Reserved.

The content contained within this book may not be reproduced, duplicated, or transmitted without direct written permission from the author or the publisher. Under no circumstances will any blame or legal responsibility be held against the publisher, or author, for any damages, reparation, or monetary loss due to the information contained within this book, either directly or indirectly.

Legal Notice: This book is copyright protected. It is only for personal use. You cannot amend, distribute, sell, use, quote or paraphrase any part, or the content within this book, without the consent of the author or publisher.

Disclaimer Notice:

Please note the information contained within this document is for educational and entertainment purposes only. All effort has been executed to present accurate, up to date, reliable, complete information. No warranties of any kind are declared or implied. Readers acknowledge that the author is not engaged in the rendering of legal, financial, medical, or professional advice. The content within this book has been derived from various sources. Please consult a licensed professional before attempting any techniques outlined in this book. By reading this document, the reader agrees that under no circumstances is the author responsible for any losses, direct or indirect, that are incurred as a result of the use of the information contained within this document, including, but not limited to, errors, omissions, or inaccuracies.

CONTENTS

Bread And Breakfast Recipes 13
- Coconut Muffins With Jalapeno 13
- Baked Eggs 13
- Cheese And Mushroom Taquitos 13
- Classical French Frittata 14
- Hot Egg Cups 14
- Pumpkin Donut Holes 14
- Simple Eggplant Spread 15
- Sausage And Cream Cheese Biscuits 15
- Breakfast Cobbler With Blueberries 15
- Vanilla French Toast Sticks 15
- Mushroom And Asparagus Frittata 16
- Creamy Broccoli Omelet 16
- Hearty Blueberry Oatmeal 16
- Frittata 17
- Hearty Cheddar Biscuits 17
- Canadian Bacon And Cheese English Muffins 17
- Banana-nut French Toast 18
- Cheddar Peppers 18
- Avocado And Egg Burrito 18
- Spinach Bacon Spread 18
- Mini Shrimp Frittata 19
- Zoodles With Cheese 19
- Shrimp And Rice Frittata 19
- Coconut Veggie And Eggs Bake 20
- Banana-pecan French Toast 20
- Ground Sausage Casserole 20
- Breakfast Granola With Cinnamon 21
- Olives And Eggs Medley 21
- Bacon And Broccoli Bread Pudding 21

Air-fried Chicken Wings And Waffles 22
Creamy Soufflés 22
Scotch Eggs 22
Cheddar Mushroom Taquitos 23
Baked Eggs With Mascarpone 23
Pita And Pepperoni Pizza 23
Scrambled Eggs With Spinach 24
Banana Bread 24
Mixed Berry Muffins 24
Scramble Casserole With Cheddar 25
Cheddar Frittata 25
Spiced Cauliflower Rice With Zucchini 25
Spinach And Mushroom Mini Quiche 26
Baked Parmesan Eggs With Kielbasa 26

Appetizers And Snacks Recipes 26
Garlic Spinach Dip 26
Sprouts Wraps Appetizer 27
Crunchy Zucchini Fries With Parmesan 27
Garlic Sesame Broccoli 27
Bacon Tater Tots 27
Cinnamon Apple Chips 28
Pigs In A Blanket 28
Delicious Zucchini Crackers 28
Garlic Cauliflower Appetizer 28
Buffalo Chicken Bites 29
Coconut-crusted Shrimp 29
Cajun Zucchini Chips 29
Crispy Vegetable Nuggets 30
Simple Curried Sweet Potato Fries 30
Flavorful Kale Chips 30
Grilled Tomatoes With Herbs 30
Mexican Potato Skins 31

- Baked Ricotta 31
- Ranch Broccoli With Cheddar 31
- Southwest Stuffed Mushrooms 32
- Hash Brown Bruschetta 32
- Jalapeño Cheese Balls 32
- Steamed Pot Stickers 33
- Tasty Shrimp Bacon Wraps 33
- Potato Pastries 33
- Zucchini And Potato Tots 34
- Crispy Phyllo Artichoke Triangles 34
- Cauliflower Wings With Buffalo Sauce 34
- Cinnamon And Sugar Peaches 34
- Rosemary Baked Cashews 35
- Spicy Chickpeas 35
- Vegetable Pot Stickers 35
- Mexican Beef Muffins With Tomato Sauce 35
- Artichoke-spinach Dip 36
- Zucchini With Parmesan Cheese 36
- Spicy Sweet Potato Fries 36
- Delectable Fish Nuggets 37
- Spinach Dip With Bread Knots 37
- Olive Oil Sweet Potato Chips 37
- Mozzarella Arancini 38
- Crispy Black Pepperoni Chips 38
- Spicy Cocktail Wieners 38
- Lemony Chicken Drumsticks 38

Vegetable Side Dishes Recipes 39

- Lush Vegetables Roast 39
- Potato-nut Casserole Dish 39
- Provolone Zucchini Balls 39
- Chermoula Beet Roast 40
- Garlicky Vegetable Rainbow Fritters 40

Bacon And Cabbage	40
Kale And Brussels Sprouts	40
Herb-roasted Vegetables	41
Air Fried Brussels Sprout	41
Tofu Bites	41
Herbed Vegetable Mélange	41
Spicy Cauliflower Roast	42
Cashew Stuffed Mushrooms	42
Cheese Spinach	42
Mint Lemon Squash	43
Potato With Creamy Cheese	43
Scalloped Mixed Vegetables	43
Sweet Potatoes With Zucchini	43
Cheese Broccoli With Basil	44
Fried Brussel Sprouts	44
Portobello Pizzas	44
Crispy Chickpeas	44
Basmati Risotto	45
Crispy Brussels Sprouts	45
Mascarpone Mushrooms	45
Savory Roasted Sweet Potatoes	46
Garlic And Sesame Carrots	46
Buttered Kale Mix	46
Kidney Beans Oatmeal In Peppers	46
Roasted Brussels Sprouts	47
Gorgonzola Mushrooms With Horseradish Mayo	47
Mashed Chives And Celery	47
Broccoli With Paprika	47
Black Bean And Tomato Chili	48
Mozzarella Veggie Tacos	48
Roasted Spiced Broccoli With Masala	48
Herbed Potatoes With Tomato Sauce	48
Creamy Cauliflower Mash	49

Herbed Radishes 49

Air Fried Potatoes With Olives 49

Lemon Fennel With Sunflower Seeds 49

Broccoli Cheese Tots 50

Roasted Bell Peppers With Garlic 50

Poultry Recipes 50

Dijon Chicken Breasts 50

Orange Chicken 51

Bacon-wrapped Chicken 51

Warm Chicken And Spinach Salad 51

Spicy Coconut Chicken Wings 52

Whole Roasted Chicken 52

Stir-fried Chicken With Mixed Fruit 53

Turkish Chicken Kebabs 53

Garlic Soy Chicken Thighs 53

Buffalo Chicken Taquitos 54

Air Fryer Naked Chicken Tenders 54

Buttermilk Country-fried Chicken Wings 54

Yellow Curry Chicken Thighs With Peanuts 55

Classical Greek Keftedes 55

Fajita Stuffed Chicken Roll-ups 55

Crunchy Chicken And Ranch Wraps 56

Healthy Vegetable Patties 56

Barbecued Chicken 56

Crispy Chicken Nuggets With Turnip 57

Classical Buffalo Wings 57

Cranberry Turkey Quesadillas 57

Fried Buffalo Chicken Taquitos 58

Dill Chicken Strips 58

Lemon Chicken In Oyster Sauce 58

Herbs Chicken Drumsticks With Tamari Sauce 59

Seasoned Chicken Breast 59

Italian Chicken And Veggies	59
Rotisserie Whole Chicken	60
Bruschetta-stuffed Chicken	60
Herbed Chicken And Broccoli	60
Apricot-glazed Turkey Tenderloin	61
Crispy Chicken Wings	61
Blackened Chicken Breasts	61
Spicy Asian Chicken Thighs With Soy Sauce	61
Chicken And Onion Sausages	62
Alfredo Chicken With Mushrooms	62
Sesame Chicken Tenders	62
Spicy And Crispy Duck	63
Chicken And Carrot	63
Chicken Fillets With Lemon Pepper & Cheddar Cheese	63
Mexican Sheet Pan Dinner	64
Grilled Chicken With Salsa Verde	64
Tex-mex Turkey Burgers	64

Beef, Pork & Lamb Recipes 65

Lamb Burger	65
Meatballs In Spicy Tomato Sauce	65
Creole Pork Chops	66
Pork Tenderloin With Bell Pepper	66
Spiced Pork Chops	66
Burgundy Beef Dish With Egg Noodles	66
Beef Taco Chimichangas	67
Spiced Lamb Kebabs	67
Best Damn Pork Chops	67
Lamb Meatballs	68
Tomato Pork Burgers	68
Mozzarella Beef Brisket	68
Steak Kabobs With Vegetables	69
Glazed Beef With Fruits	69

Cube Steak 69

Rosemary Ribeye Steaks 70

Thyme Beef Roast 70

Sizzling Beef Fajitas 70

Cajun Seasoned Bratwurst With Vegetables 70

Italian-style Cheeseburgers With Cheese Slices 71

Sweet-and-sour Polish Sausage 71

Air Fried Beef Ribs 71

Simple Rib-eye Steak 71

Roast Beef And Brown Rice 72

Vegetable Beef Meatballs With Herbs 72

Beef Chuck With Brussels Sprouts 72

Stir-fried Steak And Cabbage 73

Tasty Pork Chops 73

Asian Sirloin Steaks With Worcestershire Sauce 73

Montreal Steak 73

Sumptuous Pizza Tortilla Rolls 74

Potato And Prosciutto Salad 74

Delectable Pork Chops 74

Steak And Vegetable Skewers 74

Sweet And Spicy Pork Chops 75

Sausage, Peppers, And Onions 75

Cheese Ground Pork 75

Simple Pork Chops 76

Unstuffed Cabbage 76

Orange Pork Tenderloin 76

Ritzy Skirt Steak Fajitas 77

Pork Cutlets 77

Simple & Tasty Pork Sandwiches 78

Fish And Seafood Recipes 78

Awesome Parmesan Shrimp 78

Tex-mex Salmon Stir-fry 78

Cajun Lemon Branzino 79

Zesty Garlic Scallops 79

Tuna Veggie Stir-fry 79

Delicious Grouper Filets 79

Ginger Salmon Fillet 80

Fish And Vegetable Tacos 80

Pancetta-wrapped Scallops With Pancetta Slices 80

Easy Air Fried Salmon 80

Creamy Tuna With Zucchinis 81

Garlic Scallops With Parsley 81

Flavor Calamari With Mediterranean Sauce 81

Cajun Salmon Burgers 82

Spicy Jumbo Shrimps 82

Mustard-crusted Fish Fillets 82

Healthy Cardamom Salmon 82

Pesto Fish Finger Sandwich 83

Salmon Patty Bites 83

Beer Squid 83

Creamy Savory Salmon 84

Glazed Salmon With Soy Sauce 84

Flounder Filets With Parmesan Cheese 84

Salmon Patties 85

Crab Cakes 85

Coconut Shrimp 85

Cajun Fish Cakes 86

Parsley Saltine Fillets 86

Glazed Fillets 86

Cajun Shrimp With Veggie 86

Quick Paella 87

Healthy Salmon With Cardamom 87

Lime Trout With Parsley 87

Asian Swordfish 87

Garlic Shrimp 88

Crumbs Crusted Shrimp 88
Cilantro-lime Fried Shrimp 88
Typical Cod Nuggets 89
Fish Mania With Mustard 89
Oregano Pollock With Capers 89
Tender Salmon 90
Lemon Salmon With Chili 90
Flavored Salmon Grill With Oregano & Cumin 90

Desserts And Sweets Recipes 91

Apple-peach Crisp 91
Dark Chocolate Soufflé 91
Blueberry Muffins 91
Simple & Tasty Brownies 92
Big Chocolate Chip Cookie 92
Strawberry Cheesecake Rolls 92
S'mores 93
Donuts 93
Simple Donuts 93
Marble Cheesecake 94
Apple Peach Cranberry Crisp 94
Plum Apple Crumble With Cranberries 94
Coconut Walnuts 95
Cinnamon Sugar Donut Holes 95
Banana Chocolate Muffins 95
Curry Peaches, Pears, And Plums 96
Berry Crumble 96
Almond Cherry Bars 96
Coconut Cupcakes With Cardamom 97
Moist Cinnamon Muffins 97
Chocolate Donuts 97
Vanilla Cobbler With Hazelnut 97
Chickpea Brownies 98

Cocoa Nutmeg Cake 98

Erythritol Vanilla Butter Pie 98

Chocolate S'mores 99

Jelly Doughnuts 99

Simple Pineapple Sticks 99

Vanilla Chocolate Bites 99

Cheese Muffins With Cinnamon 100

Fudgy Chocolate Brownies 100

Honey-roasted Pears With Ricotta 100

Cardamom And Vanilla Custard 100

Lemon Butter Bars 101

Stuffed Apples 101

Chocolate Oatmeal Cookies 101

Vanilla Cookies 101

Buttery Shortbread Sticks 102

Vanilla Muffins With Pecans 102

Creamy Cheesecake Bites 102

Apple, Peach, And Cranberry Crisp 102

Pear And Apple Crisp 103

Baklava Purses 103

RECIPES INDEX 104

Bread And Breakfast Recipes

Coconut Muffins With Jalapeno

Servings: 8
Cooking Time: 15 Minutes
Ingredients:
- 5 eggs
- ⅓ cup coconut oil, melted
- 2 teaspoons baking powder
- 3 tablespoons erythritol
- 3 tablespoons jalapenos, sliced
- ¼ cup unsweetened coconut milk
- 2/3 cup coconut flour
- ¾ teaspoon salt

Directions:
1. At 325 degrees F/ 160 degrees C, preheat your air fryer.
2. In a suitable bowl, mix together coconut flour, baking powder, erythritol, and salt.
3. Add eggs, jalapenos, coconut milk, and coconut oil until well combined.
4. Pour batter into the silicone muffin molds and place into the air fryer basket.
5. Cook muffins for almost 15 minutes.
6. Serve and enjoy.

Baked Eggs

Servings: 3
Cooking Time: 10 Minutes
Ingredients:
- 3 eggs
- ½ teaspoon ground turmeric
- ¼ teaspoon salt
- 3 bacon slices
- 1 teaspoon butter, melted

Directions:
1. Using the ½ teaspoon of melted butter, grease the silicone muffin molds.
2. Place the bacon slices on the molds, shaped into circles.
3. Before cooking, heat your air fryer to 400 degrees F/ 205 degrees C.
4. Cook the bacon inside the preheated air fryer for 7 minutes.
5. When cooked, with the remaining butter brush the center of the muffins.
6. Then crack in eggs in every bacon circles.
7. To season, sprinkle with ground turmeric and salt.
8. Cook again in your air fryer for 3 minutes or more.

Cheese And Mushroom Taquitos

Servings: 8 Taquitos
Cooking Time: 40 Minutes
Ingredients:
- 8 whole-wheat tortillas
- 2–3 king oyster mushrooms
- 1 cup of shredded cheddar cheese
- 1 tablespoon of lime juice
- 1/8 cup of olive oil
- ¼ tablespoon of chili powder
- 1 teaspoon of ground cumin
- 1 teaspoon of paprika
- ½ teaspoon of dried oregano
- ½ teaspoon of garlic powder
- ¼ teaspoon of salt
- ¼ teaspoon of black pepper
- ¼ teaspoon of onion powder

Directions:
1. Clean oyster mushrooms before using. Cut them lengthwise into 1/8-inch-thick slices.
2. Mix chili, cumin, paprika, oregano, garlic, salt, pepper, and onion powder in a mixing bowl. Pour lime juice with oil and mix.
3. Place sliced mushroom into the bowl and coat with spices. Preheat your air fryer to 350°F. Bake in the air fryer for 7–10 minutes.
4. Divide the cooked mushrooms between 8 tortillas. Add shredded cheese and make a thin roll from each filled tortilla.
5. Grease all rolled tortillas with some oil and bake in the air fryer at 375°F for 10 minutes.
6. You can serve it with guacamole or pico de gallo. Enjoy your Cheese and Mushroom Taquitos!

Classical French Frittata

Servings: 3
Cooking Time: 18 Minutes
Ingredients:
- 3 eggs
- 1 tablespoon heavy cream
- 1 teaspoon Herbs de Provence
- 1 teaspoon almond butter, softened
- 2 ounces Provolone cheese, grated

Directions:
1. Before cooking, heat your air fryer to 365 degrees F/ 185 degrees C.
2. Whisk the 3 eggs together in a medium bowl and then add the heavy cream. Whisk again with a hand whisker until smooth.
3. Then add herbs de Provence and the grated cheese.
4. Gently stir the egg mixture.
5. Using almond butter, grease the baking pan.
6. Then pour the egg mixture evenly on the baking pan.
7. Cook in the preheated air fryer for 18 minutes.
8. When it has preheated, cool to room temperature, and slice and serve.

Hot Egg Cups

Servings: 6
Cooking Time: 3 Minutes
Ingredients:
- 6 eggs, beaten
- 2 jalapenos, sliced
- 2 ounces' bacon, chopped, cooked
- ½ teaspoon salt
- ½ teaspoon chili powder
- Cooking spray

Directions:
1. Spray cooking spray onto the inside of the silicone egg molds.
2. Mix up sliced jalapeno, bacon, beaten eggs, chili powder, and salt in the mixing bowl.
3. Gently whisk together the liquid and pour into the egg molds.
4. Before cooking, heat your air fryer to 400 degrees F/ 205 degrees C.
5. Place the egg cups inside the air fryer and close the air fryer.
6. Cook in your air fryer for 3 minutes.
7. Then cool the cooked cups for 2-3 minutes.
8. Remove from the silicone molds and serve.

Pumpkin Donut Holes

Servings: 12
Cooking Time: 14 Minutes
Ingredients:
- 1 cup whole-wheat pastry flour, plus more as needed
- 3 tablespoons packed brown sugar
- ½ teaspoon ground cinnamon
- 1 teaspoon low-sodium baking powder
- ⅓ cup canned no-salt-added pumpkin purée (not pumpkin pie filling; see Tip)
- 3 tablespoons 2 percent milk, plus more as needed
- 2 tablespoons unsalted butter, melted
- 1 egg white
- Powdered sugar (optional)

Directions:
1. In a medium bowl, mix the pastry flour, brown sugar, cinnamon, and baking powder.
2. In a small bowl, beat the pumpkin, milk, butter, and egg white until combined. Add the pumpkin mixture to the dry ingredients and mix until combined. You may need to add more flour or milk to form a soft dough.
3. Divide the dough into 12 pieces. With floured hands, form each piece into a ball.
4. Cut a piece of parchment paper or aluminum foil to fit inside the air fryer basket but about 1 inch smaller in diameter. Poke holes in the paper or foil and place it in the basket.
5. Put 6 donut holes into the basket, leaving some space around each. Air-fry for 5 to 7 minutes, or until the donut holes reach an internal temperature of 200°F and are firm and light golden brown.
6. Let cool for 5 minutes. Remove from the basket and roll in powdered sugar, if desired. Repeat with the remaining donut holes and serve.

Simple Eggplant Spread

Servings: 4
Cooking Time: 20 Minutes
Ingredients:
- 3 eggplants
- Salt and black pepper, to taste
- 2 tablespoons chives, chopped
- 2 tablespoons olive oil
- 2 teaspoons sweet paprika

Directions:
1. In the air fryer basket, place the eggplants.
2. Cook in your air fryer at 380 degrees F/ 195 degrees C for 20 minutes.
3. Then peel the eggplants. Place the peeled eggplants in a blender.
4. Add the remaining ingredients in the blender.
5. When it had pulsed well, remove from the blender and serve in bowls.
6. Enjoy your breakfast.

Sausage And Cream Cheese Biscuits

Servings: 5
Cooking Time: 15 Minutes
Ingredients:
- 12 ounces chicken breakfast sausage
- 1 (6-ounce) can biscuits
- ⅛ cup cream cheese

Directions:
1. Form the sausage into 5 small patties.
2. Place the sausage patties in the air fryer. Cook for 5 minutes.
3. Open the air fryer. Flip the patties. Cook for an additional 5 minutes.
4. Remove the cooked sausages from the air fryer.
5. Separate the biscuit dough into 5 biscuits.
6. Place the biscuits in the air fryer. Cook for 3 minutes.
7. Open the air fryer. Flip the biscuits. Cook for an additional 2 minutes.
8. Remove the cooked biscuits from the air fryer.
9. Split each biscuit in half. Spread 1 teaspoon of cream cheese onto the bottom of each biscuit. Top with a sausage patty and the other half of the biscuit, and serve.

Breakfast Cobbler With Blueberries

Servings: 4
Cooking Time: 15 Minutes
Ingredients:
- ⅓ cup whole-wheat pastry flour
- ¾ teaspoon baking powder
- Dash salt
- ½ cup milk
- 2 tablespoons pure maple syrup
- ½ teaspoon vanilla extract
- Cooking oil spray
- ½ cup fresh blueberries
- ¼ cup Granola, or plain store-bought granola

Directions:
1. In a suitable bowl, whisk the flour, baking powder, and salt.
2. Add maple syrup, the milk, and vanilla and gently whisk.
3. Spray a suitable 6-by-2-inch round baking pan with cooking oil and pour the prepared batter into the pan.
4. Top evenly with the blueberries and granola.
5. At 350 degrees F/ 175 degrees C, preheat your air fryer and cook for almost 15 minutes.
6. Garnish and serve.

Vanilla French Toast Sticks

Servings: 6
Cooking Time: 10 Minutes
Ingredients:
- 4 slices Texas toast
- 1 tablespoon butter
- 1 egg
- 1 teaspoon stevia
- 1 teaspoon ground cinnamon
- ¼ cup milk
- 1 teaspoon vanilla extract
- Cooking oil

Directions:
1. Cut the bread into sticks and keep them aside.
2. Beat the rest of the recipe ingredients in a suitable wide bowl.
3. At 400 degrees F/ 205 degrees C, preheat your air fryer.
4. Dip the bread sticks in the prepared egg mixture and place in the air fryer.
5. Air fry the bread sticks for 10 minutes.
6. Serve.

Mushroom And Asparagus Frittata

Servings: 4
Cooking Time: 10 Minutes
Ingredients:
- 6 eggs
- 3 mushrooms, sliced
- 10 asparagus, chopped
- ¼ cup half and half
- 2 teaspoons butter, melted
- 1 cup mozzarella cheese, shredded
- 1 teaspoon black pepper
- 1 teaspoon salt

Directions:
1. Toss mushrooms and asparagus with melted butter and add into the air fryer basket.
2. Cook mushrooms and asparagus at 350 degrees F/ 175 degrees C for 5 minutes. Shake basket twice.
3. Meanwhile, in a suitable bowl, whisk together eggs, half and half, black pepper, and salt.
4. Transfer cook mushrooms and asparagus into the air fryer basket.
5. Pour egg mixture over mushrooms and asparagus.
6. Place dish in the preheated air fryer and cook at almost 350 degrees F/ 175 degrees C for 5 minutes or until eggs are set.
7. Slice and serve.

Creamy Broccoli Omelet

Servings: 4
Cooking Time: 14 Minutes
Ingredients:
- 4 eggs, beaten
- 1 tablespoon cream cheese
- ½ teaspoon chili flakes
- ½ cup broccoli florets, chopped
- ¼ teaspoon salt
- ¼ cup heavy cream
- ¼ teaspoon white pepper
- Cooking spray

Directions:
1. In a large bowl, place the beaten eggs, salt, white pepper, and chili flakes.
2. With a hand whisker, stir together until the salt is dissolved.
3. Place the heavy cream and cream cheese in the bowl and again stir until homogenous.
4. Then add the broccoli florets.
5. Before cooking, heat your air fryer to 375 degrees F/ 190 degrees C.
6. Using cooking spray, spray the air fryer basket from inside.
7. Pour in the egg liquid and cook in the air fryer for 14 minutes.

Hearty Blueberry Oatmeal

Servings: 6
Cooking Time: 25 Minutes
Ingredients:
- 1½ cups quick oats
- 1¼ teaspoons ground cinnamon, divided
- ½ teaspoon baking powder
- Pinch salt
- 1 cup unsweetened vanilla almond milk
- ¼ cup honey
- 1 teaspoon vanilla extract
- 1 egg, beaten
- 2 cups blueberries
- Olive oil
- 1½ teapoons sugar, divided
- 6 tablespoons low-fat whipped topping (optional)

Directions:
1. In a large bowl, mix together the oats, 1 teaspoon of cinnamon, baking powder, and salt.
2. In a medium bowl, whisk together the almond milk, honey, vanilla and egg.
3. Pour the liquid ingredients into the oats mixture and stir to combine. Fold in the blueberries.
4. Lightly spray a round air fryer–friendly pan with oil.
5. Add half the blueberry mixture to the pan.
6. Sprinkle ⅛ teaspoon of cinnamon and ½ teaspoon sugar over the top.
7. Cover the pan with aluminum foil and place gently in the fryer basket.
8. Air fry for 20 minutes. Remove the foil and air fry for an additional 5 minutes. Transfer the mixture to a shallow bowl.
9. Repeat with the remaining blueberry mixture, ½ teaspoon of sugar, and ⅛ teaspoon of cinnamon.
10. To serve, spoon into bowls and top with whipped topping.

Frittata

Servings: 2 Servings
Cooking Time: 30 Minutes
Ingredients:
- 4 eggs
- ½ cup of cooked and chopped sausage
- ½ cup of shredded cheddar cheese
- 1 chopped green onion
- 2 tablespoons of chopped red bell pepper
- 1 pinch of cayenne powder

Directions:
1. Preheat your air fryer to 350°F. Lightly grease a 6-inch cake pan with some oil.
2. Whisk eggs in a large bowl. Add the sausage, bell pepper, cheese, onion, and cayenne powder, and mix until well combined.
3. Transfer the egg mixture into the prepared cake pan and cook in the air fryer at 350°F for 18–20 minutes. Check the readiness using a toothpick; it should come out clean after inserting in the center.
4. Serve with any fresh vegetables and greens. Enjoy your Frittata!

Hearty Cheddar Biscuits

Servings:8
Cooking Time: 22 Minutes
Ingredients:
- 2⅓ cups self-rising flour
- 2 tablespoons sugar
- ½ cup butter (1 stick), frozen for 15 minutes
- ½ cup grated Cheddar cheese, plus more to melt on top
- 1⅓ cups buttermilk
- 1 cup all-purpose flour, for shaping
- 1 tablespoon butter, melted

Directions:
1. Line a buttered 7-inch metal cake pan with parchment paper or a silicone liner.
2. Combine the flour and sugar in a large mixing bowl. Grate the butter into the flour. Add the grated cheese and stir to coat the cheese and butter with flour. Then add the buttermilk and stir just until you can no longer see streaks of flour. The dough should be quite wet.
3. Spread the all-purpose (not self-rising) flour out on a small cookie sheet. With a spoon, scoop 8 evenly sized balls of dough into the flour, making sure they don't touch each other. With floured hands, coat each dough ball with flour and toss them gently from hand to hand to shake off any excess flour. Put each floured dough ball into the prepared pan, right up next to the other. This will help the biscuits rise, rather than spreading out.
4. Preheat the air fryer to 380°F (193°C).
5. Transfer the cake pan to the basket of the air fryer. Let the ends of the aluminum foil sling hang across the cake pan before returning the basket to the air fryer.
6. Air fry for 20 minutes. Check the biscuits twice to make sure they are not getting too brown on top. If they are, re-arrange the aluminum foil strips to cover any brown parts. After 20 minutes, check the biscuits by inserting a toothpick into the center of the biscuits. It should come out clean. If it needs a little more time, continue to air fry for two extra minutes. Brush the tops of the biscuits with some melted butter and sprinkle a little more grated cheese on top if desired. Pop the basket back into the air fryer for another 2 minutes.
7. Remove the cake pan from the air fryer. Let the biscuits cool for just a minute or two and then turn them out onto a plate and pull apart. Serve immediately.

Canadian Bacon And Cheese English Muffins

Servings: 4
Cooking Time: 10 Minutes
Ingredients:
- 4 English muffins
- 8 slices Canadian bacon
- 4 slices cheese
- Cooking oil

Directions:
1. Split each English muffin. Assemble the breakfast sandwiches by layering 2 slices of Canadian bacon and 1 slice of cheese onto each English muffin bottom. Top with the other half of the English muffin.
2. Place the sandwiches in the air fryer. Spray the top of each with cooking oil. Cook for 4 minutes.
3. Open the air fryer and flip the sandwiches. Cook for an additional 4 minutes.
4. Cool before serving.

Banana-nut French Toast

Servings: 8 Toasts
Cooking Time: 25 Minutes
Ingredients:
- 8 slices of whole-grain bread
- ¾ cup of any milk you like
- 1 sliced banana
- 1 cup of rolled oats
- 1 cup of pecan, walnuts, or any other nuts
- 2 tablespoons of ground flax seeds (optional)
- 1 teaspoon of cinnamon

Directions:
1. Preheat your air fryer to 350°F.
2. Put nuts, oats, cinnamon, and flax seeds into a food processor and pulse until it will look like bread crumbs. Transfer it into a wide shallow plate.
3. Pour milk into a dip bowl. Soak 1–2 pieces of bread for 15 seconds on one side, then turn it over and continue soaking for an extra 15 seconds. Transfer the soaked pieces to the oat-nut mixture and coat with it from both sides.
4. Place the prepared bread slices into the air fryer basket in one layer. Cook them at 350°F for 3 minutes, flip, and continue cooking for 3 more minutes.
5. Repeat steps 3 and 4 with the remaining bread slices.
6. Serve with maple syrup and banana slices. Enjoy your Banana-Nut French Toast!

Cheddar Peppers

Servings: 4
Cooking Time: 20 Minutes
Ingredients:
- ½ cup cheddar cheese, shredded
- 2 tablespoons chives, chopped
- A pinch of salt and black pepper
- ¼ cup coconut cream
- 1 cup red bell peppers, chopped
- Cooking spray

Directions:
1. Grease a suitable baking pan with cooking spray.
2. Mix shredded cheddar cheese, chopped chives, salt, black pepper, coconut cream, and the chopped red bell peppers in a medium bowl.
3. Pour the mixture in the greased pan.
4. Cook in your air fryer at 360 degrees F/ 180 degrees C for 20 minutes.
5. When the cooking time is up, serve warm on plates.

Avocado And Egg Burrito

Servings: 4
Cooking Time: 3 To 5 Minutes
Ingredients:
- 2 hardboiled egg whites, chopped
- 1 hardboiled egg, chopped
- 1 avocado, peeled, pitted, and chopped
- 1 red bell pepper, chopped
- 3 tablespoons low-sodium salsa, plus additional for serving (optional)
- 1 (1.2-ounce) slice low-sodium, low-fat American cheese, torn into pieces
- 4 low-sodium whole-wheat flour tortillas (see Tip)

Directions:
1. In a medium bowl, thoroughly mix the egg whites, egg, avocado, red bell pepper, salsa, and cheese.
2. Place the tortillas on a work surface and evenly divide the filling among them. Fold in the edges and roll up. Secure the burritos with toothpicks if necessary.
3. Put the burritos in the air fryer basket. Air-fry for 3 to 5 minutes, or until the burritos are light golden brown and crisp. Serve with more salsa (if using).

Spinach Bacon Spread

Servings: 4
Cooking Time: 10 Minutes
Ingredients:
- 2 tablespoons coconut cream
- 3 cups spinach leaves
- 2 tablespoons cilantro
- 2 tablespoons bacon, cooked and crumbled
- Salt and black pepper to the taste

Directions:
1. Combine coconut cream, spinach leaves, salt, and black pepper in a suitable baking pan.
2. Transfer the baking pan into your air fryer and cook at 360 degrees F/ 180 degrees C for 10 minutes.
3. When cooked, transfer to a blender and pulse well.
4. To serve, sprinkle the bacon on the top of the mixture.

Mini Shrimp Frittata

Servings: 4
Cooking Time: 20 Minutes
Ingredients:
- 1 teaspoon olive oil, plus more for spraying
- ½ small red bell pepper, finely diced
- 1 teaspoon minced garlic
- 1 (4-ounce) can of tiny shrimp, drained
- Salt
- Freshly ground black pepper
- 4 eggs, beaten
- 4 teaspoons ricotta cheese

Directions:
1. Spray four ramekins with olive oil.
2. In a medium skillet over medium-low heat, heat 1 teaspoon of olive oil. Add the bell pepper and garlic and sauté until the pepper is soft, about 5 minutes
3. Add the shrimp, season with salt and pepper, and cook until warm, 1 to 2 minutes. Remove from the heat.
4. Add the eggs and stir to combine.
5. Pour one quarter of the mixture into each ramekin.
6. Place 2 ramekins in the fryer basket and cook for 6 minutes.
7. Remove the fryer basket from the air fryer and stir the mixture in each ramekin. Top each fritatta with 1 teaspoon of ricotta cheese. Return the fryer basket to the air fryer and cook until eggs are set and the top is lightly browned, 4 to 5 minutes.
8. Repeat with the remaining two ramekins.

Zoodles With Cheese

Servings: 3
Cooking Time: 45 Minutes
Ingredients:
- 1 egg
- ½ cup parmesan cheese, grated
- ½ cup feta cheese, crumbled
- 1 tablespoon thyme
- 1 garlic clove, chopped
- 1 onion, chopped
- 2 medium zucchinis, trimmed and spiralized
- 2 tablespoon olive oil
- 1 cup mozzarella cheese, grated
- ½ teaspoon black pepper
- ½ teaspoon salt

Directions:
1. At 350 degrees F/ 175 degrees C, preheat your air fryer.
2. Add spiralized zucchini and salt in a colander and set aside for almost 10 minutes.
3. Wash zucchini noodles and pat dry with a paper towel.
4. Set a suitable pan with oil over medium heat.
5. Add garlic and onion and sauté for 3-4 minutes
6. Stir in zucchini noodles and cook for 4-5 minutes or until softened.
7. Add zucchini mixture into the air fryer basket.
8. Stir in egg, thyme, cheeses. Mix well and season.
9. Place pan in the preheated air fryer and cook for 30-35 minutes.
10. Serve and enjoy.

Shrimp And Rice Frittata

Servings: 4
Cooking Time: 15 Minutes
Ingredients:
- 4 eggs
- Pinch salt
- ½ teaspoon dried basil
- Nonstick cooking spray
- ½ cup cooked rice
- ½ cup chopped cooked shrimp
- ½ cup baby spinach
- ½ cup grated Monterey Jack or Cojack cheese

Directions:
1. In a small bowl, beat the eggs with the salt and basil until frothy. Spray a 6-by-6-by-2-inch pan with nonstick cooking spray.
2. Combine the rice, shrimp, and spinach in the prepared pan. Pour the eggs in and sprinkle with the cheese.
3. Bake for 14 to 18 minutes or until the frittata is puffed and golden brown.

Coconut Veggie And Eggs Bake

Servings: 6
Cooking Time: 30 Minutes
Ingredients:
- Cooking spray
- 2 cups green and red bell pepper, chopped
- 2 spring onions, chopped
- 1 teaspoon thyme, chopped
- Salt and black pepper to the taste
- 1 cup coconut cream
- 4 eggs, whisked
- 1 cup cheddar cheese, grated

Directions:
1. Place all the ingredients except the cooking spray and cheese in a mixing bowl and mix up to combine.
2. Using the cooking spray to grease a suitable pan.
3. Pour the eggs mixture and bell peppers evenly on your pan.
4. Sprinkle the top with the cheese.
5. Transfer the pan inside your air fryer and close the air fryer.
6. Cook the coconut veggie and eggs bake at 350 degrees F/ 175 degrees C for 30 minutes.
7. When cooked, transfer onto plates and serve for breakfast.

Banana-pecan French Toast

Servings: 8
Cooking Time: 10 Minutes
Ingredients:
- 8 slices of whole-grain bread
- ¾ cup of any milk you like
- 1 sliced banana
- 1 cup of rolled oats
- 1 cup of pecan, chopped
- 2 tablespoons of ground flax seeds
- 1 teaspoon of cinnamon

Directions:
1. At 350 degrees F/ 175 degrees C, preheat your air fryer.
2. Mix nuts, cinnamon, oats, and flax seeds into a food processor and pulse until crumbly.
3. Pour milk into a deep and wide bowl.
4. Soak 1–2 pieces of bread for almost 15-30 seconds per side.
5. Transfer the soaked bread pieces to the oats mixture and cover with it from per side.
6. Set the prepared soak bread slices into the air fryer basket in 1 layer.
7. Cook them at 350 degrees F/ 175 degrees C for 3 minutes, flip, and continue cooking for 3 more minutes.
8. Repeat the same steps with the remaining bread slices.
9. Serve with maple syrup and banana slices.
10. Enjoy your Banana-Nut French Toast!

Ground Sausage Casserole

Servings: 6 Servings
Cooking Time: 30 Minutes
Ingredients:
- 4 eggs
- 1 pound of ground sausage
- 1 pound of hash browns
- 1 diced yellow bell pepper
- 1 diced green bell pepper
- 1 diced red bell pepper
- ¼ cup of diced onion
- Pinch of salt and black pepper, to taste

Directions:
1. Preheat your air fryer to 355°F. Grease a cake pan with some oil.
2. First, put the hash browns on the bottom of the cake pan, then spread the uncooked sausage, sprinkle salt and black pepper. Cover it with onions and peppers.
3. Bake in the air fryer at 355°F for 10 minutes.
4. Meanwhile, whisk eggs with seasonings in a mixing bowl. Pour the egg mixture over the top of the casserole and continue cooking for 10 more minutes.
5. Serve warm and enjoy your Ground Sausage Casserole!

Breakfast Granola With Cinnamon

Servings: 2.
Cooking Time: 40 Minutes
Ingredients:
- 1 cup rolled oats
- 3 tablespoons pure maple syrup
- 1 tablespoon sugar
- 1 tablespoon neutral-flavored oil
- ¼ teaspoon salt
- ¼ teaspoon ground cinnamon
- ¼ teaspoon vanilla extract

Directions:
1. In a suitable bowl, stir together the oats, maple syrup, sugar, oil, salt, cinnamon, and vanilla until thoroughly combined.
2. Transfer the granola to a 6-by-2-inch round baking pan.
3. Once your air fryer unit is preheated, place the pan into the basket.
4. At 250 degrees F/ 120 degrees C, heat your air fryer in advance and cook for almost 40 minutes.
5. Serve.

Olives And Eggs Medley

Servings: 4
Cooking Time: 20 Minutes
Ingredients:
- 2 cups black olives, pitted and chopped
- 4 eggs, whisked
- ¼ teaspoon sweet paprika
- 1 tablespoon cilantro, chopped
- ½ cup cheddar, shredded
- A pinch of salt and black pepper
- Cooking spray

Directions:
1. Add the olives into the beaten egg in a bowl and mix together all the ingredients except the cooking spray.
2. At 350 degrees F/ 175 degrees C, heat your air fryer in advance.
3. Grease your baking pan with the cooking spray.
4. Pour the olive-egg mixture evenly in the pan.
5. Transfer the pan inside your air fryer and cook for 20 minutes.
6. Serve the medley on plates. Enjoy your breakfast.

Bacon And Broccoli Bread Pudding

Servings:4
Cooking Time: 48 Minutes
Ingredients:
- ½ pound (227 g) thick cut bacon, cut into ¼-inch pieces
- 3 cups brioche bread, cut into ½-inch cubes
- 2 tablespoons butter, melted
- 3 eggs
- 1 cup milk
- ½ teaspoon salt
- Freshly ground black pepper, to taste
- 1 cup frozen broccoli florets, thawed and chopped
- 1½ cups grated Swiss cheese

Directions:
1. Preheat the air fryer to 400°F (204°C).
2. Air fry the bacon for 8 minutes until crispy, shaking the basket a few times to help it air fry evenly. Remove the bacon and set it aside on a paper towel.
3. Air fry the brioche bread cubes for 2 minutes to dry and toast lightly.
4. Butter a cake pan. Combine all the ingredients in a large bowl and toss well. Transfer the mixture to the buttered cake pan, cover with aluminum foil and refrigerate the bread pudding overnight, or for at least 8 hours.
5. Remove the cake pan from the refrigerator an hour before you plan to bake and let it sit on the countertop to come to room temperature.
6. Preheat the air fryer to 330°F (166°C). Transfer the covered cake pan to the basket of the air fryer, lowering the pan into the basket. Fold the ends of the aluminum foil over the top of the pan before returning the basket to the air fryer.
7. Air fry for 20 minutes. Remove the foil and air fry for an additional 20 minutes. If the top browns a little too much before the custard has set, simply return the foil to the pan. The bread pudding has cooked through when a skewer inserted into the center comes out clean.
8. Serve warm.

Air-fried Chicken Wings And Waffles

Servings: 4
Cooking Time: 20 Minutes
Ingredients:
- 8 whole chicken wings
- 1 teaspoon garlic powder
- Chicken seasoning or rub
- Black pepper
- ½ cup all-purpose flour
- Cooking oil
- 8 frozen waffles
- Maple syrup

Directions:
1. At 400 degrees F/ 205 degrees C, preheat your air fryer.
2. In a suitable bowl, spice the chicken with the garlic powder and chicken seasoning and black pepper to flavor.
3. Put the chicken to a sealable plastic bag and add the flour. Shake to thoroughly coat the chicken.
4. Grease its air fryer basket with cooking oil.
5. Place chicken in the greased air fryer basket and air fry for 20 minutes while tossing occasionally.
6. Transfer the air fried chicken wings to a plate and add frozen waffles to the air fryer and cook for almost 6 minutes.
7. Serve the air fried chicken with waffles.

Creamy Soufflés

Servings: 8
Cooking Time: 20 Minutes
Ingredients:
- 6 large eggs, separated
- ¾ cup heavy cream
- ¼ teaspoon cayenne pepper
- ½ teaspoon xanthan gum
- ½ teaspoon black pepper
- ¼ teaspoon cream of tartar
- 2 tablespoons chives, chopped
- 2 cups cheddar cheese, shredded
- 1 teaspoon salt

Directions:
1. At 325 degrees F/ 160 degrees C, preheat your air fryer.
2. Spray eight ramekins with cooking spray. Set aside.
3. In a suitable bowl, whisk together almond flour, cayenne pepper, black pepper, salt, and xanthan gum.
4. Slowly add heavy cream and mix to combine.
5. Whisk in egg yolks, chives, and cheese until well combined.
6. In a suitable bowl, add egg whites and cream of tartar and beat until stiff peaks form.
7. Fold egg white mixture into the dry almond flour mixture until combined.
8. Pour mixture into the prepared ramekins. Divide ramekins in batches.
9. Place the first batch of ramekins into the air fryer basket.
10. Cook soufflé for 20 minutes.
11. Serve and enjoy.

Scotch Eggs

Servings: 6
Cooking Time: 12 Minutes
Ingredients:
- 6 hard-cooked eggs
- 1½ pounds bulk lean chicken or turkey sausage
- 3 raw eggs, divided
- 1½ cups dried bread crumbs, divided
- ½ cup flour
- Oil, for misting

Directions:
1. Peel the hard-cooked eggs and set aside.
2. In a large bowl, combine the chicken sausage, one raw egg, and ½ cup of the bread crumbs, and mix well. Divide into six pieces and flatten each into a long oval.
3. In a shallow bowl, beat the remaining two raw eggs.
4. Roll each hard-cooked egg in the flour and wrap one of the chicken sausage pieces around the egg to completely encircle it.
5. Roll the egg first in the flour, then dip in the beaten eggs, and finally dip in the bread crumbs to coat. Prepare the remaining eggs the same way.
6. Place the eggs in a single layer in the air fryer and spray with oil.
7. Air-fry for 6 minutes, then turn using tongs and mist with more oil. Air-fry for 5 to 7 minutes or until the chicken is thoroughly cooked and the Scotch eggs are brown.
8. Did You Know? You can buy hard-cooked eggs, already peeled, at many grocery stores! Look for them in the dairy case, and make sure to follow expiration dates to the letter. Or hard-cook them right in your air fryer (Hard-Cooked Eggs, here).

Cheddar Mushroom Taquitos

Servings: 8
Cooking Time: 20 Minutes
Ingredients:
- 8 whole-wheat tortillas
- 2–3 king oyster mushrooms
- 1 cup of shredded cheddar cheese
- 1 tablespoon of lime juice
- ⅛ cup of olive oil
- ¼ tablespoon of chili powder
- 1 teaspoon of ground cumin
- 1 teaspoon of paprika
- ½ teaspoon of dried oregano
- ½ teaspoon of garlic powder
- ¼ teaspoon of salt
- ¼ teaspoon of black pepper
- ¼ teaspoon of onion powder

Directions:
1. Clean oyster mushrooms before using.
2. Cut them lengthwise into ⅛-inch-thick slices.
3. Mix chili, cumin, paprika, oregano, garlic, salt, black pepper, and onion powder in a suitable mixing bowl.
4. Add lime juice with oil and mix.
5. Place sliced mushroom into the bowl and rub with spices.
6. At 350 degrees F/ 175 degrees C, preheat your air fryer.
7. Air fry the mushroom in the air fryer for 7–10 minutes almost.
8. Divide the cooked mushrooms between all the tortillas.
9. Add shredded cheese and make a thin roll from each stuffed tortilla.
10. Spray all rolled tortillas with some oil and Air fry for almost 10 minutes.
11. Serve.

Baked Eggs With Mascarpone

Servings: 2
Cooking Time: 3 Minutes
Ingredients:
- 2 eggs
- 1 teaspoon mascarpone
- ¼ teaspoon ground nutmeg
- ¼ teaspoon dried basil
- ¼ teaspoon dried oregano
- ¼ teaspoon dried cilantro
- ¼ teaspoon ground turmeric
- ¼ teaspoon onion powder
- ¼ teaspoon salt

Directions:
1. In a mixing bowl, whisk in the eggs.
2. Stir with mascarpone until homogenous.
3. Then add all spices and gently mix up the liquid.
4. Pour the liquid into the silicone egg molds.
5. Place on the air fryer basket.
6. Cook the baked eggs with mascarpone in your air fryer at 400 degrees F/ 205 degrees C for 3 minutes.

Pita And Pepperoni Pizza

Servings: 1
Cooking Time: 6 Minutes
Ingredients:
- 1 teaspoon olive oil
- 1 tablespoon pizza sauce
- 1 pita bread
- 6 pepperoni slices
- ¼ cup grated Mozzarella cheese
- ¼ teaspoon garlic powder
- ¼ teaspoon dried oregano

Directions:
1. Preheat the air fryer to 350°F (177°C). Grease the air fryer basket with olive oil.
2. Spread the pizza sauce on top of the pita bread. Put the pepperoni slices over the sauce, followed by the Mozzarella cheese.
3. Season with garlic powder and oregano.
4. Put the pita pizza inside the air fryer and place a trivet on top.
5. Bake in the preheated air fryer for 6 minutes and serve.

Scrambled Eggs With Spinach

Servings: 4
Cooking Time: 20 Minutes
Ingredients:
- 1 tablespoon olive oil
- ½ teaspoon smoked paprika
- 12 eggs, whisked
- 3 cups baby spinach
- Salt and black pepper to the taste

Directions:
1. Mix together smoked paprika, eggs, spinach, salt, and pepper in a bowl until whisk well.
2. Grease a suitable pan that fits in your air fryer.
3. Transfer inside the air fryer and preheat your air fryer to 360 degrees F/ 180 degrees C.
4. When it has preheated, mix the spinach mix and eggs in the pan.
5. Close the air fryer and cook for 20 minutes.
6. Serve on plates.

Banana Bread

Servings: 3
Cooking Time: 22 Minutes
Ingredients:
- 3 ripe bananas, mashed
- 1 cup sugar
- 1 large egg
- 4 tablespoons (½ stick) unsalted butter, melted
- 1½ cups all-purpose flour
- 1 teaspoon baking soda
- 1 teaspoon salt

Directions:
1. Coat the insides of 3 mini loaf pans with cooking spray.
2. In a large mixing bowl, mix the bananas and sugar.
3. In a separate large mixing bowl, combine the egg, butter, flour, baking soda, and salt and mix well.
4. Add the banana mixture to the egg and flour mixture. Mix well.
5. Divide the batter evenly among the prepared pans.
6. Preheat the air fryer to 310°F (154°C). Set the mini loaf pans into the air fryer basket.
7. Bake in the preheated air fryer for 22 minutes. Insert a toothpick into the center of each loaf; if it comes out clean, they are done.
8. When the loaves are cooked through, remove the pans from the air fryer basket. Turn out the loaves onto a wire rack to cool.
9. Serve warm.

Mixed Berry Muffins

Servings: 8
Cooking Time: 15 Minutes
Ingredients:
- 1⅓ cups plus 1 tablespoon flour
- 2 teaspoons baking powder
- ¼ cup white sugar
- 2 tablespoons brown sugar
- 2 eggs
- ⅔ cup whole milk
- ⅓ cup safflower oil
- 1 cup mixed fresh berries

Directions:
1. In medium bowl, combine the 1⅓ cups flour, baking powder, white sugar, and brown sugar, and mix well.
2. In small bowl, combine the eggs, milk, and oil, and beat until combined. Stir the egg mixture into the dry ingredients just until combined.
3. In another small bowl, toss the mixed berries with the remaining 1 tablespoon of flour until coated. Stir gently into the batter.
4. Double up 16 foil muffin cups to make 8 cups. Put 4 cups into the air fryer and fill three-quarters full with the batter. Bake for 12 to 17 minutes or until the tops of the muffins spring back when lightly touched with your finger.
5. Repeat with the remaining muffin cups and batter. Cool on a wire rack for 10 minutes before serving.
6. Did You Know? You can use frozen berries in this recipe, but don't thaw them before use. If frozen berries are thawed they will make the batter too wet, and the berries may stain the batter.

Scramble Casserole With Cheddar

Servings: 4
Cooking Time: 15 Minutes
Ingredients:
- 6 slices bacon
- 6 eggs
- Salt
- Black pepper
- Cooking oil
- ½ cup chopped red bell pepper
- ½ cup chopped green bell pepper
- ½ cup chopped onion
- ¾ cup shredded Cheddar cheese

Directions:
1. At 400 degrees F/ 205 degrees C, preheat your air fryer.
2. In a suitable pan, over medium-high heat, cook the bacon, 5 to 7 minutes, flipping too evenly crisp.
3. Dry out on paper towels, crumble, and set aside. In a suitable bowl, whisk the eggs.
4. Add black pepper and salt to taste.
5. Grease a suitable barrel pan with cooking oil.
6. Add the beaten eggs, crumbled bacon, red bell pepper, green bell pepper, and onion to the pan.
7. Place this pan in the air fryer. Cook for 6 minutes more.
8. Drizzle the cheese over the casserole.
9. Cook for an additional 2 minutes. Cool before serving.

Cheddar Frittata

Servings: 2
Cooking Time: 20 Minutes
Ingredients:
- 4 eggs
- ½ cup of cooked and chopped sausage
- ½ cup of shredded cheddar cheese
- 1 chopped green onion
- 2 tablespoons of chopped red bell pepper
- 1 pinch of cayenne powder

Directions:
1. At 350 degrees F/ 175 degrees C, preheat your air fryer.
2. Lightly grease a suitable 6-inch cake pan with some oil or cooking spray.
3. Whisk eggs in a suitable bowl.
4. Add the sausage, bell pepper, onion, cheese, and cayenne powder, and stir until well combined.
5. Transfer the prepared egg mixture into the cake pan and cook in the preheated air fryer almost 20 minutes.
6. Serve with any fresh vegetables and greens. Enjoy your Frittata!

Spiced Cauliflower Rice With Zucchini

Servings: 2
Cooking Time: 25 Minutes
Ingredients:
- 1 cauliflower head, cut into florets
- ½ teaspoon cumin
- ½ teaspoon chili powder
- 6 onion spring, chopped
- 2 jalapenos, chopped
- 4 tablespoons olive oil
- 1 zucchini, trimmed and cut into cubes
- ½ teaspoon paprika
- ½ teaspoon garlic powder
- ½ teaspoon cayenne pepper
- ½ teaspoon black pepper
- ½ teaspoon salt

Directions:
1. At 370 degrees F/ 185 degrees C, preheat your Air fryer.
2. Grind cauliflower florets into the food processor.
3. Transfer cauliflower rice into the air fryer basket and drizzle with ½ oil.
4. Place pan in the preheated air fryer and cook for 12 minutes, stir halfway through.
5. Add the remaining oil in a small pan and heat over medium heat.
6. Add zucchini and cook for 5-8 minutes
7. Stir in jalapenos and onion then sauté for 5 minutes
8. Add spices and stir well. Set aside.
9. Stir in cauliflower rice in the zucchini mixture and stir well.
10. Serve and enjoy.

Spinach And Mushroom Mini Quiche

Servings: 4
Cooking Time: 15 Minutes
Ingredients:
- 1 teaspoon olive oil, plus more for spraying
- 1 cup coarsely chopped mushrooms
- 1 cup fresh baby spinach, shredded
- 4 eggs, beaten
- ½ cup shredded Cheddar cheese
- ½ cup shredded mozzarella cheese
- ¼ teaspoon salt
- ¼ teaspoon black pepper

Directions:
1. Spray 4 silicone baking cups with olive oil and set aside.
2. In a medium sauté pan over medium heat, warm 1 teaspoon of olive oil. Add the mushrooms and sauté until soft, 3 to 4 minutes.
3. Add the spinach and cook until wilted, 1 to 2 minutes. Set aside.
4. In a medium bowl, whisk together the eggs, Cheddar cheese, mozzarella cheese, salt, and pepper.
5. Gently fold the mushrooms and spinach into the egg mixture.
6. Pour ¼ of the mixture into each silicone baking cup.
7. Place the baking cups into the fryer basket and air fry for 5 minutes. Stir the mixture in each ramekin slightly and air fry until the egg has set, an additional 3 to 5 minutes.

Baked Parmesan Eggs With Kielbasa

Servings: 4
Cooking Time: 8 Minutes
Ingredients:
- 4 eggs
- 1 tablespoon heavy cream
- 1 ounce Parmesan, grated
- 1 teaspoon dried parsley
- 3 ounces kielbasa, chopped
- 1 teaspoon coconut oil

Directions:
1. Add the coconut oil in a suitable baking pan and melt it in your air fryer at 385 degrees F/ 195 degrees C for about 2 to 3 minutes.
2. At the same time in a mixing bowl, whisk the eggs and add heavy cream and the dried parsley.
3. Whisk them together.
4. Add the chopped kielbasa in the melted coconut oil.
5. Cook at 385 degrees F/ 195 degrees C for 4 minutes.
6. When cooked, add Parmesan and the whisked egg mixture and use a fork to stir them together.
7. Cook for 4 or more minutes, halfway through cooking scramble the mixture.

Appetizers And Snacks Recipes

Garlic Spinach Dip

Servings: 8
Cooking Time: 20 Minutes
Ingredients:
- 8 ounces cream cheese, softened
- ¼ teaspoon garlic powder
- ½ cup onion, minced
- ⅓ cup water chestnuts, drained and chopped
- 1 cup mayonnaise
- 1 cup parmesan cheese, grated
- 1 cup frozen spinach, thawed and squeeze out all liquid
- ½ teaspoon black pepper

Directions:
1. Grease its air fryer basket with cooking spray.
2. Add all the recipe ingredients into the bowl and mix until well combined.
3. Transfer bowl mixture into the prepared baking dish and place dish in air fryer basket.
4. Cook at almost 300 degrees F/ 150 degrees C for 35-40 minutes. After 20 minutes of cooking stir dip.
5. Serve and enjoy.

Sprouts Wraps Appetizer

Servings: 12
Cooking Time: 20 Minutes
Ingredients:
- 12 bacon strips
- 12 Brussels sprouts
- A drizzle of olive oil

Directions:
1. Use a bacon strip to wrap each Brussels.
2. Brush the wraps with olive oil before arranging them to the air fryer basket.
3. Cook the wraps for 20 minutes at 350 degrees F/ 175 degrees C.
4. When done, serve as an appetizer.

Crunchy Zucchini Fries With Parmesan

Servings: 4
Cooking Time: 10 Minutes
Ingredients:
- 2 medium zucchinis, cut into fry shape
- ½ teaspoon garlic powder
- 1 teaspoon Italian seasoning
- ½ cup parmesan cheese, grated
- ½ cup almond flour
- 1 egg, lightly beaten
- Black pepper
- Salt

Directions:
1. Add egg in a suitable bowl and whisk well.
2. In a shallow bowl, mix together almond flour, spices, parmesan cheese, black pepper, and salt.
3. Grease its air fryer basket with cooking spray.
4. Dip those zucchini fries in egg then coat with almond flour mixture and place in the air fryer basket.
5. Cook zucchini fries for almost 10 minutes at 400 degrees F/ 205 degrees C.
6. Serve and enjoy.

Garlic Sesame Broccoli

Servings: 4
Cooking Time: 20 Minutes
Ingredients:
- 1 large head broccoli
- ½ lemon, juiced
- 3 garlic cloves, minced
- 1 tablespoon coconut oil
- 1 tablespoon white sesame seeds
- 2 teaspoons Maggi sauce or other seasonings to taste

Directions:
1. Wash and dry the broccoli. Chop it up into small florets.
2. Place the minced garlic in your air fryer basket, along with the coconut oil, lemon juice and Maggi sauce.
3. Heat for 2 minutes at 320 degrees F/ 160 degrees C and give it a stir.
4. Put the garlic and broccoli in the basket and cook for another 13 minutes.
5. Top the broccoli with the white sesame seeds and resume cooking for 5 more minutes, ensuring the seeds become nice and toasty.

Bacon Tater Tots

Servings: 4
Cooking Time: 17 Minutes
Ingredients:
- 24 frozen tater tots
- 6 slices precooked bacon
- 2 tablespoons maple syrup
- 1 cup shredded Cheddar cheese

Directions:
1. Put the tater tots in the air fryer basket. Air-fry for 10 minutes, shaking the basket halfway through the cooking time.
2. Meanwhile, cut the bacon into 1-inch pieces and shred the cheese.
3. Remove the tater tots from the air fryer basket and put into a 6-by-6-by-2-inch pan. Top with the bacon and drizzle with the maple syrup. Air-fry for 5 minutes or until the tots and bacon are crisp.
4. Top with the cheese and air-fry for 2 minutes or until the cheese is melted.

Cinnamon Apple Chips

Servings: 4
Cooking Time: 10 Minutes
Ingredients:
- Olive oil
- 2 apples, any variety, cored, cut in half, and cut into thin slices
- 2 heaped teaspoons ground cinnamon

Directions:
1. Spray a fryer basket lightly with oil.
2. In a medium bowl, toss the apple slices with the cinnamon until evenly coated.
3. Place the apple slices in the fryer basket in a single layer. You may need to cook them in batches.
4. Air fry for 4 to 5 minutes. Shake the basket and cook until crispy, another 4 to 5 minutes.

Pigs In A Blanket

Servings: 6
Cooking Time: 14 Minutes
Ingredients:
- 24 cocktail smoked sausages
- 6 slices deli-sliced Cheddar cheese, each cut into 8 rectangular pieces
- 1 (8-ounce / 227-g) tube refrigerated crescent roll dough

Directions:
1. Preheat the air fryer to 350°F (177°C).
2. Unroll the crescent roll dough into one large sheet. If your crescent roll dough has perforated seams, pinch or roll all the perforated seams together. Cut the large sheet of dough into 4 rectangles. Then cut each rectangle into 6 pieces by making one slice lengthwise in the middle and 2 slices horizontally. You should have 24 pieces of dough.
3. Make a deep slit lengthwise down the center of the cocktail sausage. Stuff two pieces of cheese into the slit in the sausage. Roll one piece of crescent dough around the stuffed cocktail sausage, leaving the ends of the sausage exposed. Pinch the seam together. Repeat with the remaining sausages.
4. Air fry in 2 batches for 7 minutes, placing the sausages seam-side down in the basket. Serve hot.

Delicious Zucchini Crackers

Servings: 12
Cooking Time: 20 Minutes
Ingredients:
- 1 cup zucchini, grated
- 2 tablespoons flax meal
- 1 teaspoon salt
- 3 tablespoons almond flour
- ¼ teaspoon baking powder
- ¼ teaspoon chili flakes
- 1 tablespoon xanthan gum
- 1 tablespoon butter, softened
- 1 egg, beaten
- Cooking spray

Directions:
1. Squeeze the zucchini to remove the vegetable juice and transfer to a large bowl.
2. Thoroughly mix up the flax meal, salt, almond flour, baking powder, chili flakes and xanthan gum.
3. Add butter and egg. Knead the non-sticky dough.
4. Place the mixture on the baking paper and cover with another baking paper.
5. Roll up the dough into the flat square.
6. After this, remove the baking paper from the dough surface.
7. Cut it on medium size crackers.
8. Prepare the air fryer basket by lining it with baking paper, and then put the crackers inside it.
9. Spray them with cooking spray. Cook them for 20 minutes at 355 degrees F/ 180 degrees C.
10. Serve and enjoy.

Garlic Cauliflower Appetizer

Servings: 2
Cooking Time: 20 Minutes
Ingredients:
- 5 cups cauliflower florets
- ½ teaspoon Kosher salt
- ½ teaspoon paprika
- ½ teaspoon garlic powder
- 2 tablespoons avocado oil

Directions:
1. Prepare a large bowl, add the Kosher salt, avocado oil, paprika, garlic powder, and cauliflower florets. Coat well.
2. Arrange the coated cauliflower to the basket of your air fryer and cook at 390 degrees F/ 200 degrees C for 18 minutes, shaking the basket halfway through.
3. Cooking in batches is suggested.
4. When done, serve immediately. Bon appétit!

Buffalo Chicken Bites

Servings: 4
Cooking Time: 14 To 18 Minutes
Ingredients:
- ⅔ cup sour cream
- ¼ cup creamy blue cheese salad dressing
- ¼ cup crumbled blue cheese
- 1 celery stalk, finely chopped
- 1 pound chicken tenders, cut into thirds crosswise
- 3 tablespoons Buffalo chicken wing sauce
- 1 cup panko bread crumbs
- 2 tablespoons olive oil

Directions:
1. In a small bowl, combine the sour cream, salad dressing, blue cheese, and celery, and set aside.
2. In a medium bowl, combine the chicken pieces and Buffalo wing sauce and stir to coat. Let sit while you get the bread crumbs ready.
3. Combine the bread crumbs and olive oil on a plate and mix.
4. Coat the chicken pieces in the bread crumb mixture, patting each piece so the crumbs adhere.
5. Air-fry in batches for 7 to 9 minutes, shaking the basket once, until the chicken is cooked to 165°F and is golden brown. Serve with the blue cheese sauce on the side.
6. Did You Know? Buffalo chicken wings were first invented in the Anchor Bar in Buffalo, New York, when the owner needed to serve a lot of appetizers in a hurry. They became an immediate hit and the flavor—a combination of a spicy hot sauce with cool blue cheese—is now a classic.

Coconut-crusted Shrimp

Servings: 4
Cooking Time: 4 Minutes
Ingredients:
- ½ pound (227 g) medium shrimp, peeled and deveined (tails intact)
- 1 cup canned coconut milk
- Finely grated zest of 1 lime
- Kosher salt, to taste
- ½ cup panko bread crumbs
- ½ cup unsweetened shredded coconut
- Freshly ground black pepper, to taste
- Cooking spray
- 1 small or ½ medium cucumber, halved and deseeded
- 1 cup coconut yogurt
- 1 serrano chile, deseeded and minced

Directions:
1. Preheat the air fryer to 400°F (204°C).
2. In a bowl, combine the shrimp, coconut milk, lime zest, and ½ teaspoon kosher salt. Let the shrimp stand for 10 minutes.
3. Meanwhile, in a separate bowl, stir together the bread crumbs and shredded coconut and season with salt and pepper.
4. A few at a time, add the shrimp to the bread crumb mixture and toss to coat completely. Transfer the shrimp to a wire rack set over a baking sheet. Spray the shrimp all over with cooking spray.
5. Transfer the shrimp to the air fryer and air fry for 4 minutes, or until golden brown and cooked through. Transfer the shrimp to a serving platter and season with more salt.
6. Grate the cucumber into a small bowl. Stir in the coconut yogurt and chile and season with salt and pepper. Serve alongside the shrimp while they're warm.

Cajun Zucchini Chips

Servings: 4
Cooking Time: 15 Minutes
Ingredients:
- Olive oil
- 2 large zucchini, cut into ⅛-inch-thick slices
- 2 teaspoons Cajun seasoning

Directions:
1. Spray a fryer basket lightly with olive oil.
2. Put the zucchini slices in a medium bowl and spray them generously with olive oil.
3. Sprinkle the Cajun seasoning over the zucchini and stir to make sure they are evenly coated with oil and seasoning.
4. Place slices in a single layer in the fryer basket, making sure not to overcrowd. You will need to cook these in several batches.
5. Air fry for 8 minutes. Flip the slices over and air fry until they are as crisp and brown as you prefer, an additional 7 to 8 minutes.

Crispy Vegetable Nuggets

Servings: 4
Cooking Time: 10 Minutes
Ingredients:
- 1 zucchini, chopped roughly
- ½ of carrot, chopped roughly
- 1 cup all-purpose flour
- 1 egg
- 1 cup panko breadcrumbs
- 1 tablespoon garlic powder
- ½ tablespoon mustard powder
- 1 tablespoon onion powder
- Black pepper and salt, to taste

Directions:
1. At 380 degrees F/ 195 degrees C, preheat your air fryer and grease its air fryer basket.
2. Put zucchini, carrot, mustard powder, garlic powder, onion powder, black pepper and salt in a food processor and pulse until combined.
3. Place the dry flour in a shallow dish and whisk the eggs with milk in a second dish.
4. Place breadcrumbs in a third shallow dish.
5. Coat the vegetable nuggets evenly in flour and dip in the egg mixture.
6. Roll into the breadcrumbs evenly and arrange the nuggets in an air fryer basket.
7. Cook for about 10 minutes and dish out to serve warm.

Simple Curried Sweet Potato Fries

Servings: 3
Cooking Time: 20 Minutes
Ingredients:
- 2 small sweet potatoes, peel and cut into fry shape
- ¼ teaspoon coriander
- ½ teaspoon curry powder
- 2 tablespoons olive oil
- ¼ teaspoon salt

Directions:
1. Add all the recipe ingredients into the suitable mixing bowl and toss well.
2. Grease its air fryer basket with cooking spray.
3. Transfer sweet potato fries in the air fryer basket.
4. Cook for 20 minutes at 370 degrees F/ 185 degrees C. Shake halfway through.
5. Serve and enjoy.

Flavorful Kale Chips

Servings: 4
Cooking Time: 5 Minutes
Ingredients:
- 4 cups kale, stemmed
- 1 tablespoon nutritional yeast flakes
- 2 teaspoons ranch seasoning
- 2 tablespoons olive oil
- ¼ teaspoon salt

Directions:
1. Add all the recipe ingredients into the suitable mixing bowl and toss well.
2. Grease its air fryer basket with cooking spray.
3. Add kale in air fryer basket and cook for 4-5 minutes at 370 degrees F/ 185 degrees C.
4. Serve and enjoy.

Grilled Tomatoes With Herbs

Servings: 2
Cooking Time: 20 Minutes
Ingredients:
- 2 tomatoes, medium to large
- Herbs of your choice, to taste
- Black pepper to taste
- High quality cooking spray

Directions:
1. Wash and dry the tomatoes, before chopping them in half.
2. Lightly spritz them all over with cooking spray.
3. Season each ½ with oregano, basil, parsley, rosemary, thyme, sage, etc. as desired and black pepper.
4. Put the halves in the tray of your air fryer. Cook for 20 minutes at 320 degrees F/ 160 degrees C.
5. Serve.

Mexican Potato Skins

Servings: 6
Cooking Time: 55 Minutes
Ingredients:
- Olive oil
- 6 medium russet potatoes, scrubbed
- Salt
- Freshly ground black pepper
- 1 cup fat-free refried black beans
- 1 tablespoon taco seasoning
- ½ cup salsa
- ¾ cup reduced-fat shredded Cheddar cheese

Directions:
1. Spray a fryer basket lightly with olive oil.
2. Spray the potatoes lightly with oil and season with salt and pepper. Pierce each potato a few times with a fork.
3. Place the potatoes in the fryer basket. Air fry until fork tender, 30 to 40 minutes. The cooking time will depend on the size of the potatoes. You can cook the potatoes in the microwave or a standard oven, but they won't get the same lovely crispy skin they will get in the air fryer.
4. While the potatoes are cooking, in a small bowl, mix together the beans and taco seasoning. Set aside until the potatoes are cool enough to handle.
5. Cut each potato in half lengthwise. Scoop out most of the insides, leaving about ¼ inch in the skins so the potato skins hold their shape.
6. Season the insides of the potato skins with salt and black pepper. Lightly spray the insides of the potato skins with oil. You may need to cook them in batches.
7. Place them into the fryer basket, skin side down, and air fry until crisp and golden, 8 to 10 minutes.
8. Transfer the skins to a work surface and spoon ½ tablespoon of seasoned refried black beans into each one. Top each with 2 teaspoons salsa and 1 tablespoon shredded Cheddar cheese.
9. Place filled potato skins in the fryer basket in a single layer. Lightly spray with oil.
10. Air fry until the cheese is melted and bubbly, 2 to 3 minutes.

Baked Ricotta

Servings: 2
Cooking Time: 15 Minutes
Ingredients:
- 1 (15-ounce / 425-g) container whole milk Ricotta cheese
- 3 tablespoons grated Parmesan cheese, divided
- 2 tablespoons extra-virgin olive oil
- 1 teaspoon chopped fresh thyme leaves
- 1 teaspoon grated lemon zest
- 1 clove garlic, crushed with press
- ¼ teaspoon salt
- ¼ teaspoon pepper
- Toasted baguette slices or crackers, for serving

Directions:
1. Preheat the air fryer to 380°F (193°C).
2. To get the baking dish in and out of the air fryer, create a sling using a 24-inch length of foil, folded lengthwise into thirds.
3. Whisk together the Ricotta, 2 tablespoons of the Parmesan, oil, thyme, lemon zest, garlic, salt, and pepper. Pour into a baking dish. Cover the dish tightly with foil.
4. Place the sling under dish and lift by the ends into the air fryer, tucking the ends of the sling around the dish. Bake for 10 minutes. Remove the foil cover and sprinkle with the remaining 1 tablespoon of the Parmesan. Air fry for 5 more minutes, or until bubbly at edges and the top is browned.
5. Serve warm with toasted baguette slices or crackers.

Ranch Broccoli With Cheddar

Servings: 6
Cooking Time: 35 Minutes
Ingredients:
- 4 cups broccoli florets
- ¼ cup ranch dressing
- ½ cup sharp cheddar cheese, shredded
- ¼ cup heavy whipping cream
- Kosher black pepper and salt to taste

Directions:
1. At 375 degrees F/ 190 degrees C preheat your air fryer.
2. In a suitable bowl, combine all of the recipe ingredients until the broccoli is well-covered.
3. In a casserole dish, spread out the broccoli mixture.
4. Air fry for 30 minutes.
5. Take out of your fryer and mix.
6. If the florets are not tender, Air fry for another 5 minutes until tender.
7. Serve!

Southwest Stuffed Mushrooms

Servings: 4
Cooking Time: 8 To 12 Minutes
Ingredients:
- 16 medium button mushrooms, rinsed and patted dry
- ⅓ cup low-sodium salsa
- 3 garlic cloves, minced
- 1 medium onion, finely chopped
- 1 jalapeño pepper, minced (see Tip)
- ⅛ teaspoon cayenne pepper
- 3 tablespoons shredded pepper Jack cheese
- 2 teaspoons olive oil

Directions:
1. Remove the stems from the mushrooms and finely chop them, reserving the whole caps.
2. In a medium bowl, mix the salsa, garlic, onion, jalapeño, cayenne, and pepper Jack cheese. Stir in the chopped mushroom stems.
3. Stuff this mixture into the mushroom caps, mounding the filling. Drizzle the olive oil on the mushrooms. Air-fry the mushrooms in the air fryer basket for 8 to 12 minutes, or until the filling is hot and the mushrooms are tender. Serve immediately.

Hash Brown Bruschetta

Servings: 4
Cooking Time: 6 To 8 Minutes
Ingredients:
- 4 frozen hash brown patties
- 1 tablespoon olive oil
- ⅓ cup chopped cherry tomatoes
- 3 tablespoons diced fresh mozzarella
- 2 tablespoons grated Parmesan cheese
- 1 tablespoon balsamic vinegar
- 1 tablespoon minced fresh basil

Directions:
1. Place the hash brown patties in the air fryer in a single layer. Air-fry for 6 to 8 minutes or until the potatoes are crisp, hot, and golden brown.
2. Meanwhile, combine the olive oil, tomatoes, mozzarella, Parmesan, vinegar, and basil in a small bowl.
3. When the potatoes are done, carefully remove from the basket and arrange on a serving plate. Top with the tomato mixture and serve.
4. Did You Know? Bruschetta comes from the word that means "to roast over coals," and refers to the toasted bread. It has many incarnations, including a recipe made by simply rubbing the warm little toasts with a cut clove of fresh garlic.

Jalapeño Cheese Balls

Servings: 12
Cooking Time: 15 Minutes
Ingredients:
- 4 ounces cream cheese
- ⅓ cup shredded mozzarella cheese
- ⅓ cup shredded Cheddar cheese
- 2 jalapeños, finely chopped
- ½ cup bread crumbs
- 2 eggs
- ½ cup all-purpose flour
- Salt
- Pepper
- Cooking oil

Directions:
1. In a medium bowl, combine the cream cheese, mozzarella, Cheddar, and jalapeños. Mix well.
2. Form the cheese mixture into balls about an inch thick. Using a small ice cream scoop works well.
3. Arrange the cheese balls on a sheet pan and place in the freezer for 15 minutes. This will help the cheese balls maintain their shape while frying.
4. Spray the air fryer basket with cooking oil.
5. Place the bread crumbs in a small bowl. In another small bowl, beat the eggs. In a third small bowl, combine the flour with salt and pepper to taste, and mix well.
6. Remove the cheese balls from the freezer. Dip the cheese balls in the flour, then the eggs, and then the bread crumbs.
7. Place the cheese balls in the air fryer. (It is okay to stack them.) Spray with cooking oil. Cook for 8 minutes.
8. Open the air fryer and flip the cheese balls. I recommend flipping them instead of shaking so the balls maintain their form. Cook an additional 4 minutes.
9. Cool before serving.

Steamed Pot Stickers

Servings: 30
Cooking Time: 10 Minutes
Ingredients:
- ½ cup finely chopped cabbage
- ¼ cup finely chopped red bell pepper
- 2 green onions, finely chopped
- 1 egg, beaten
- 2 tablespoons cocktail sauce
- 2 teaspoons low-sodium soy sauce
- 30 wonton wrappers
- 3 tablespoons water, plus more for brushing the wrappers

Directions:
1. In a small bowl, combine the cabbage, pepper, green onions, egg, cocktail sauce, and soy sauce, and mix well.
2. Put about 1 teaspoon of the mixture in the center of each wonton wrapper. Fold the wrapper in half, covering the filling; dampen the edges with water, and seal. You can crimp the edges of the wrapper with your fingers so they look like the pot stickers you get in restaurants. Brush them with water.
3. Put 3 tablespoons water in the pan under the air fryer basket. Cook the pot stickers in 2 batches for 9 to 10 minutes or until the pot stickers are hot and the bottoms are lightly browned.

Tasty Shrimp Bacon Wraps

Servings: 8-10
Cooking Time: 8 Minutes
Ingredients:
- ½ teaspoon red pepper flakes, crushed
- 1 tablespoon salt
- 1 teaspoon chili powder
- 1 ¼ pounds shrimp, peeled and deveined
- 1 teaspoon paprika
- ½ teaspoon black pepper, ground
- 1 tablespoon shallot powder
- ¼ teaspoon cumin powder
- 1 ¼ pounds thin bacon slices

Directions:
1. Prepare your clean air fryer.
2. Preheat the air fryer for 4 to 5 minutes at 360 degrees F/ 180 degrees C.
3. Oil or spray the air-frying basket gently.
4. Mix the shrimp and seasoning in a medium-size bowl thoroughly, until they are coated well.
5. Use a slice of bacon to wrap around the shrimps and use a toothpick to secure them. Then place them in the refrigerator and cool for 30 minutes.
6. Add the shrimps to the basket and then put the basket in the air fryer.
7. Cook the shrimps for 8 minutes.
8. You can serve with cocktail sticks or your choice of dip (optional).

Potato Pastries

Servings: 8
Cooking Time: 37 Minutes
Ingredients:
- 2 large potatoes, peeled
- 1 tablespoon olive oil
- ½ cup carrot, peeled and chopped
- ½ cup onion, chopped
- 2 garlic cloves, minced
- 1 tablespoon fresh ginger, minced
- ½ cup green peas, shelled
- Salt and ground black pepper, as needed
- 3 puff pastry sheets

Directions:
1. Boil water in a suitable pan, then put the potatoes and cook for about 15-20 minutes
2. Drain the potatoes well and then mash the potatoes.
3. Heat the oil over medium heat in a skillet, then add the carrot, onion, ginger, garlic and sauté for about 4-5 minutes.
4. Then drain all the fat from the skillet.
5. Stir in the mashed potatoes, peas, salt and black pepper. Continue to cook for about 1-2 minutes.
6. Remove the potato mixture from heat and set aside to cool completely.
7. After placing the puff pastry onto a smooth surface, cut each puff pastry sheet into four pieces and cut each piece into a round shape.
8. Add about 2 tablespoons of veggie filling over each pastry round.
9. Use your wet finger to moisten the edges.
10. To seal the filling, fold each pastry round in half.
11. Firmly press the edges with a fork.
12. Set the temperature setting to 390 degrees F/ 200 degrees C.
13. Arrange the pastries in the basket of your air fryer and air fry for about 5 minutes at 390 minutes.
14. Work in 2 batches.
15. Serve.

Zucchini And Potato Tots

Servings: 4
Cooking Time: 20 Minutes
Ingredients:
- 1 large zucchini, grated
- 1 medium baked potato, skin removed and mashed
- ¼ cup shredded Cheddar cheese
- 1 large egg, beaten
- ½ teaspoon kosher salt
- Cooking spray

Directions:
1. Preheat the air fryer to 390°F (199°C).
2. Wrap the grated zucchini in a paper towel and squeeze out any excess liquid, then combine the zucchini, baked potato, shredded Cheddar cheese, egg, and kosher salt in a large bowl.
3. Spray a baking pan with cooking spray, then place individual tablespoons of the zucchini mixture in the pan and air fry for 10 minutes. Repeat this process with the remaining mixture.
4. Remove the tots and allow to cool on a wire rack for 5 minutes before serving.

Crispy Phyllo Artichoke Triangles

Servings: 18
Cooking Time: 9 To 12 Minutes
Ingredients:
- ¼ cup Ricotta cheese
- 1 egg white
- ⅓ cup minced and drained artichoke hearts
- 3 tablespoons grated Mozzarella cheese
- ½ teaspoon dried thyme
- 6 sheets frozen phyllo dough, thawed
- 2 tablespoons melted butter

Directions:
1. Preheat the air fryer to 400°F (204°C).
2. In a small bowl, combine the Ricotta cheese, egg white, artichoke hearts, Mozzarella cheese, and thyme, and mix well.
3. Cover the phyllo dough with a damp kitchen towel while you work so it doesn't dry out. Using one sheet at a time, place on the work surface and cut into thirds lengthwise.
4. Put about 1½ teaspoons of the filling on each strip at the base. Fold the bottom right-hand tip of phyllo over the filling to meet the other side in a triangle, then continue folding in a triangle. Brush each triangle with butter to seal the edges. Repeat with the remaining phyllo dough and filling.
5. Place the triangles in the air fryer basket. Bake, 6 at a time, for about 3 to 4 minutes, or until the phyllo is golden brown and crisp.
6. Serve hot.

Cauliflower Wings With Buffalo Sauce

Servings: 4
Cooking Time: 14 Minutes
Ingredients:
- 1 cauliflower head, cut into florets
- 1 tablespoon butter, melted
- ½ cup buffalo sauce
- Black pepper
- Salt

Directions:
1. Grease its air fryer basket with cooking spray.
2. In a suitable bowl, mix together buffalo sauce, butter, black pepper, and salt.
3. Add cauliflower florets into the air fryer basket and cook at almost 400 degrees F/ 205 degrees C for 7 minutes.
4. Transfer cauliflower florets into the buffalo sauce mixture and toss well.
5. Again, add cauliflower florets into the air fryer basket and cook for 7 minutes more at 400 degrees F/ 205 degrees C.
6. Serve and enjoy.

Cinnamon And Sugar Peaches

Servings: 4
Cooking Time: 13 Minutes
Ingredients:
- Olive oil
- 2 tablespoons sugar
- ¼ teaspoon ground cinnamon
- 4 peaches, cut into wedges

Directions:
1. Spray a fryer basket lightly with olive oil.
2. In a medium bowl, combine the sugar and cinnamon. Add the peaches and toss to coat evenly.
3. Place the peaches in a single layer in the fryer basket on their sides. You may need to cook them in batches.
4. Air fry for 5 minutes. Turn the peaches skin side down, lightly spray them with oil, and air fry until the peaches are lightly brown and caramelized, 5 to 8 more minutes.

Rosemary Baked Cashews

Servings: 2
Cooking Time: 3 Minutes
Ingredients:
- 2 sprigs of fresh rosemary (1 chopped and 1 whole)
- 1 teaspoon olive oil
- 1 teaspoon kosher salt
- ½ teaspoon honey
- 2 cups roasted and unsalted whole cashews
- Cooking spray

Directions:
1. Preheat the air fryer to 300°F (149°C).
2. In a medium bowl, whisk together the chopped rosemary, olive oil, kosher salt, and honey. Set aside.
3. Spray the air fryer basket with cooking spray, then place the cashews and the whole rosemary sprig in the basket and bake for 3 minutes.
4. Remove the cashews and rosemary from the air fryer, then discard the rosemary and add the cashews to the olive oil mixture, tossing to coat.
5. Allow to cool for 15 minutes before serving.

Spicy Chickpeas

Servings: 4
Cooking Time: 20 Minutes
Ingredients:
- Olive oil
- ½ teaspoon ground cumin
- ½ teaspoon chili powder
- ¼ teaspoon cayenne pepper
- ¼ teaspoon salt
- 1 (19-ounce) can chickpeas, drained and rinsed

Directions:
1. Spray a fryer basket lightly with olive oil.
2. In a small bowl, combine the cumin, chili powder, cayenne pepper, and salt.
3. In a medium bowl, add the chickpeas and lightly spray them with olive oil. Add the spice mixture and toss until coated evenly.
4. Transfer the chickpeas to the fryer basket. Air fry until the chickpeas reach your desired level of crunchiness, 15 to 20 minutes, making sure to shake the basket every 5 minutes.

Vegetable Pot Stickers

Servings: 12
Cooking Time: 11 To 18 Minutes
Ingredients:
- 1 cup shredded red cabbage
- ¼ cup chopped button mushrooms
- ¼ cup grated carrot
- 2 tablespoons minced onion
- 2 garlic cloves, minced
- 2 teaspoons grated fresh ginger
- 12 gyoza/pot sticker wrappers (see Tip)
- 2½ teaspoons olive oil, divided

Directions:
1. In a 6-by-2-inch pan, combine the red cabbage, mushrooms, carrot, onion, garlic, and ginger. Add 1 tablespoon of water. Place in the air fryer and cook for 3 to 6 minutes, until the vegetables are crisp-tender. Drain and set aside.
2. Working one at a time, place the pot sticker wrappers on a work surface. Top each wrapper with a scant 1 tablespoon of the filling. Fold half of the wrapper over the other half to form a half circle. Dab one edge with water and press both edges together.
3. To another 6-by-2-inch pan, add 1¼ teaspoons of olive oil. Put half of the pot stickers, seam-side up, in the pan. Air-fry for 5 minutes, or until the bottoms are light golden brown. Add 1 tablespoon of water and return the pan to the air fryer.
4. Air-fry for 4 to 6 minutes more, or until hot. Repeat with the remaining pot stickers, remaining 1¼ teaspoons of oil, and another tablespoon of water. Serve immediately.

Mexican Beef Muffins With Tomato Sauce

Servings: 4
Cooking Time: 15 Minutes
Ingredients:
- 1 cup ground beef
- 1 teaspoon taco seasonings
- 2 oz. Mexican blend cheese, shredded
- 1 teaspoon tomato sauce
- Cooking spray

Directions:
1. Thoroughly mix up ground beef and taco seasonings in a mixing bowl.
2. Spray the muffin molds with cooking spray.
3. Transfer the ground beef mixture in the muffin molds. Place the cheese and tomato sauce on the top.
4. Transfer the muffin molds in the prepared air fryer and cook them for 15 minutes at 375 degrees F/ 190 degrees C.
5. When cooked, serve and enjoy.

Artichoke-spinach Dip

Servings: 3
Cooking Time: 10 Minutes
Ingredients:
- 1 (14-ounce / 397-g) can artichoke hearts packed in water, drained and chopped
- 1 (10-ounce / 284-g) package frozen spinach, thawed and drained
- 1 teaspoon minced garlic
- 2 tablespoons mayonnaise
- ¼ cup nonfat plain Greek yogurt
- ¼ cup shredded part-skim Mozzarella cheese
- ¼ cup grated Parmesan cheese
- ¼ teaspoon freshly ground black pepper
- Cooking spray

Directions:
1. Preheat the air fryer to 360°F (182°C).
2. Wrap the artichoke hearts and spinach in a paper towel and squeeze out any excess liquid, then transfer the vegetables to a large bowl.
3. Add the minced garlic, mayonnaise, plain Greek yogurt, Mozzarella, Parmesan, and black pepper to the large bowl, stirring well to combine.
4. Spray a baking pan with cooking spray, then transfer the dip mixture to the pan and air fry for 10 minutes.
5. Remove the dip from the air fryer and allow to cool in the pan on a wire rack for 10 minutes before serving.

Zucchini With Parmesan Cheese

Servings: 6
Cooking Time: 30 Minutes
Ingredients:
- 6 medium zucchini, cut into sticks
- 6 tablespoons Parmesan cheese, grated
- 4 egg whites, beaten
- ½-teaspoon garlic powder
- 1 cup bread crumbs
- Pepper to taste
- Salt to taste

Directions:
1. At 400 degrees F/ 205 degrees C, heat your air fryer in advance.
2. Mix up the beaten egg whites with some salt and pepper in a suitable bowl.
3. In another bowl, add the garlic powder, bread crumbs, and Parmesan cheese and combine well.
4. Before rolling in the bread crumbs, dredge each zucchini stick in the egg whites.
5. Place the coated zucchini in the basket of your air fryer and for 20 minutes at 400 degrees F/ 205 degrees C.

Spicy Sweet Potato Fries

Servings: 4
Cooking Time: 8 To 12 Minutes
Ingredients:
- 2 large sweet potatoes, peeled and cut into ⅓-by-⅓-inch sticks
- 1 teaspoon ground cumin
- 1 teaspoon ground paprika
- ½ teaspoon garlic powder
- ½ teaspoon cayenne pepper
- ⅛ teaspoon freshly ground black pepper
- 1 cup low-fat Greek yogurt
- 2 teaspoons olive oil

Directions:
1. In a medium bowl of cold water, soak the sweet potato sticks and set them aside while you make the dip.
2. In a small bowl, mix the cumin, paprika, garlic powder, cayenne, and black pepper.
3. In another small bowl, whisk half the spice mixture with the yogurt. Refrigerate.
4. Drain the sweet potatoes, pat them dry, and place them in a large bowl. Sprinkle them with the olive oil. Toss for 1 minute to coat thoroughly.
5. Sprinkle the fries with the remaining spice mixture and toss again to coat. Transfer the potatoes to the air fryer basket. Air-fry for 8 to 12 minutes, or until crisp, hot, and golden brown, shaking the basket once during cooking.
6. Transfer to a serving dish. Serve with the dip.

Delectable Fish Nuggets

Servings: 4
Cooking Time: 10 Minutes
Ingredients:
- 1 cup all-purpose flour
- 2 eggs
- ¾ cup breadcrumbs
- 1 lb. cod, cut into 1x2½-inch strips
- Pinch of salt
- 1 tablespoon olive oil

Directions:
1. At 380 degrees F/ 195 degrees C, heat your air fryer in advance and grease an Air fryer basket.
2. In a shallow dish, place the dish, and whisk the eggs in another dish.
3. In the third shallow dish, mix up the breadcrumbs, salt and oil.
4. Let the fish strips be coated evenly in flour and dip in the egg.
5. Roll into the breadcrumbs evenly and arrange the nuggets in the basket of your air fryer.
6. Cook for about 10 minutes at 380 degrees F/ 195 degrees C.
7. When the time is up, dish out to serve warm.

Spinach Dip With Bread Knots

Servings: 6
Cooking Time: 16 To 21 Minutes
Ingredients:
- Nonstick cooking spray
- 1 (8-ounce) package cream cheese, cut into cubes
- ¼ cup sour cream
- ½ cup frozen chopped spinach, thawed and drained
- ½ cup grated Swiss cheese
- 2 green onions, chopped
- ½ (11-ounce) can refrigerated breadstick dough
- 2 tablespoons melted butter
- 3 tablespoons grated Parmesan cheese

Directions:
1. Spray a 6-by-6-by-2-inch pan with nonstick cooking spray.
2. In a medium bowl, combine the cream cheese, sour cream, spinach, Swiss cheese, and green onions, and mix well. Spread into the prepared pan and bake for 8 minutes or until hot.
3. While the dip is baking, unroll six of the breadsticks and cut them in half crosswise to make 12 pieces.
4. Gently stretch each piece of dough and tie into a loose knot; tuck in the ends.
5. When the dip is hot, remove from the air fryer and carefully place each bread knot on top of the dip, covering the surface of the dip. Brush each knot with melted butter and sprinkle Parmesan cheese on top.
6. Bake for 8 to 13 minutes or until the bread knots are golden brown and cooked through.

Olive Oil Sweet Potato Chips

Servings: 5
Cooking Time: 20 Minutes
Ingredients:
- 3 sweet potatoes
- 2 teaspoons extra-virgin olive oil
- 1 teaspoon cinnamon (optional)
- Salt
- Pepper

Directions:
1. Peel the sweet potatoes using a vegetable peeler. Cut the potatoes crosswise into thin slices. You can also use a mandoline to slice the potatoes into chips.
2. Place the sweet potatoes in a large bowl of cold water for 30 minutes. This helps remove the starch from the sweet potatoes, which promotes crisping.
3. Drain the sweet potatoes. Dry the slices thoroughly with paper towels or napkins.
4. Place the sweet potatoes in another large bowl. Drizzle with the olive oil and sprinkle with the cinnamon, if using, and salt and pepper to taste. Toss to fully coat.
5. Place the sweet potato slices in the air fryer. It is okay to stack them, but do not overcrowd. You may need to cook the chips in two batches. Cook the potatoes for 10 minutes.
6. Open the air fryer and shake the basket. Cook the chips for an additional 10 minutes.
7. Cool before serving.

Mozzarella Arancini

Servings: 16
Cooking Time: 8 To 11 Minutes
Ingredients:
- 2 cups cooked rice, cooled
- 2 eggs, beaten
- 1½ cups panko bread crumbs, divided
- ½ cup grated Parmesan cheese
- 2 tablespoons minced fresh basil
- 16 ¾-inch cubes Mozzarella cheese
- 2 tablespoons olive oil

Directions:
1. Preheat the air fryer to 400°F (204°C).
2. In a medium bowl, combine the rice, eggs, ½ cup of the bread crumbs, Parmesan cheese, and basil. Form this mixture into 16 1½-inch balls.
3. Poke a hole in each of the balls with your finger and insert a Mozzarella cube. Form the rice mixture firmly around the cheese.
4. On a shallow plate, combine the remaining 1 cup of the bread crumbs with the olive oil and mix well. Roll the rice balls in the bread crumbs to coat.
5. Air fry the arancini in batches for 8 to 11 minutes or until golden brown.
6. Serve hot.

Crispy Black Pepperoni Chips

Servings: 6
Cooking Time: 8 Minutes
Ingredients:
- 6 ounces black pepperoni slices

Directions:
1. Place 1 batch of black pepperoni slices in the air fryer basket.
2. Cook for 8 minutes at 360 degrees F/ 180 degrees C.
3. Cook remaining black pepperoni slices using same steps.
4. Serve and enjoy.

Spicy Cocktail Wieners

Servings: 4
Cooking Time: 15 Minutes
Ingredients:
- 1 lb. pork cocktail sausages
- For the Sauce:
- ¼ cup mayonnaise
- ¼ cup cream cheese
- 1 whole grain mustard
- ¼- ½ teaspoon balsamic vinegar
- 1 garlic clove, finely minced
- ¼ teaspoon chili powder

Directions:
1. Pork the sausages a few times with a fork, them place them on the cooking pan of your air fryer.
2. Cook the sausages at 390 degrees F/ 200 degrees C for 15 minutes;
3. After 8 minutes of cooking, turn the sausages over and resume cooking.
4. Check for doneness and take the sausages out of the machine.
5. At the same time, thoroughly combine all the ingredients for the sauce.
6. Serve with warm sausages and enjoy!

Lemony Chicken Drumsticks

Servings: 2
Cooking Time: 30 Minutes
Ingredients:
- 2 teaspoons freshly ground coarse black pepper
- 1 teaspoon baking powder
- ½ teaspoon garlic powder
- 4 chicken drumsticks (4 ounces / 113 g each)
- Kosher salt, to taste
- 1 lemon

Directions:
1. In a small bowl, stir together the pepper, baking powder, and garlic powder. Place the drumsticks on a plate and sprinkle evenly with the baking powder mixture, turning the drumsticks so they're well coated. Let the drumsticks stand in the refrigerator for at least 1 hour or up to overnight.
2. Preheat the air fryer to 375°F (191°C).
3. Sprinkle the drumsticks with salt, then transfer them to the air fryer, standing them bone-end up and leaning against the wall of the air fryer basket. Air fry for 30 minutes, or until cooked through and crisp on the outside.
4. Transfer the drumsticks to a serving platter and finely grate the zest of the lemon over them while they're hot. Cut the lemon into wedges and serve with the warm drumsticks.

Vegetable Side Dishes Recipes

Lush Vegetables Roast

Servings: 6
Cooking Time: 20 Minutes
Ingredients:
- 1⅓ cups small parsnips, peeled and cubed
- 1⅓ cups celery
- 2 red onions, sliced
- 1⅓ cups small butternut squash, cut in half, deseeded and cubed
- 1 tablespoon fresh thyme needles
- 1 tablespoon olive oil
- Salt and ground black pepper, to taste

Directions:
1. Preheat the air fryer to 390°F (199°C).
2. Combine the cut vegetables with the thyme, olive oil, salt and pepper.
3. Put the vegetables in the basket and transfer the basket to the air fryer.
4. Roast for 20 minutes, stirring once throughout the roasting time, until the vegetables are nicely browned and cooked through.
5. Serve warm.

Potato-nut Casserole Dish

Servings: 4
Cooking Time: 30 Minutes
Ingredients:
- 3 pounds sweet potatoes; scrubbed
- ¼ cup milk
- 2 tablespoons white flour
- ¼ teaspoon allspice; ground
- ½ teaspoon nutmeg; ground
- Salt to the taste
- For the topping:
- ½ cup almond flour
- ½ cup walnuts; soaked, drained and ground
- ¼ cup sugar
- 1 teaspoon cinnamon powder
- 5 tablespoons butter
- ¼ cup pecans; soaked, drained and ground
- ¼ cup coconut; shredded
- 1 tablespoon chia seeds

Directions:
1. Place potatoes in your air fryer basket, prick them with a fork and cook at almost 360 degrees F/ 180 degrees C, for 30 minutes.
2. Meanwhile; in a bowl, mix almond flour with pecans, walnuts, ¼ cup coconut, ¼ cup sugar, chia seeds, 1 teaspoon cinnamon and the butter and stir everything.
3. Transfer potatoes to a cutting board, cool them, peel and place them in a baking dish that fits your air fryer.
4. Add milk, flour, salt, nutmeg and allspice and stir
5. Add crumble mix you've made earlier on top; place dish in your air fryer's basket and Cook at almost 400 degrees F/ 205 degrees C, for almost 8 minutes.
6. Divide among plates and serve as a side dish.

Provolone Zucchini Balls

Servings: 4
Cooking Time: 12 Minutes
Ingredients:
- ¼ teaspoon salt
- ¼ teaspoon ground cumin
- 1 zucchini, grated
- 2 ounces Provolone cheese, grated
- ¼ teaspoon chili flakes
- 1 egg, beaten
- ¼ cup coconut flour
- 1 teaspoon sunflower oil

Directions:
1. Mix ground cumin, zucchini, Provolone cheese, egg, chili flakes, and salt together.
2. Make them into small balls with a spoon.
3. Line baking paper over the air fryer basket. Brush the bottom of the baking paper with sunflower oil.
4. Cook in your air fryer at 375 degrees F/ 190 degrees C for 12 minutes.
5. To avoid burning, shake the balls every 2 minutes.

Chermoula Beet Roast

Servings: 4
Cooking Time: 25 Minutes
Ingredients:
- Chermoula:
- 1 cup packed fresh cilantro leaves
- ½ cup packed fresh parsley leaves
- 6 cloves garlic, peeled
- 2 teaspoons smoked paprika
- 2 teaspoons ground cumin
- 1 teaspoon ground coriander
- ½ to 1 teaspoon cayenne pepper
- Pinch of crushed saffron (optional)
- ½ cup extra-virgin olive oil
- Kosher salt, to taste
- Beets:
- 3 medium beets, trimmed, peeled, and cut into 1-inch chunks
- 2 tablespoons chopped fresh cilantro
- 2 tablespoons chopped fresh parsley

Directions:
1. In a food processor, combine the cilantro, parsley, garlic, paprika, cumin, coriander, and cayenne. Pulse until coarsely chopped. Add the saffron, if using, and process until combined. With the food processor running, slowly add the olive oil in a steady stream; process until the sauce is uniform. Season with salt.
2. Preheat the air fryer to 375°F (191°C).
3. In a large bowl, drizzle the beets with ½ cup of the chermoula to coat. Arrange the beets in the air fryer basket. Roast for 25 to minutes, or until the beets are tender.
4. Transfer the beets to a serving platter. Sprinkle with the chopped cilantro and parsley and serve.

Garlicky Vegetable Rainbow Fritters

Servings: 2
Cooking Time: 12 Minutes
Ingredients:
- 1 zucchini, grated and squeezed
- 1 cup corn kernels
- ½ cup canned green peas
- 4 tablespoons all-purpose flour
- 2 tablespoons fresh shallots, minced
- 1 teaspoon fresh garlic, minced
- 1 tablespoon peanut oil
- Salt and black pepper, to taste
- 1 teaspoon cayenne pepper

Directions:
1. In a suitable mixing bowl, thoroughly combine all the recipe ingredients until everything is well incorporated.
2. Shape the mixture into patties.
3. Grease its air fryer basket with cooking spray.
4. Cook the patties in the preheated air fryer at about 365 degrees F/ 185 degrees C for 6 minutes almost.
5. Flip and cook for a 6 minutes more.
6. Serve immediately and enjoy!

Bacon And Cabbage

Servings: 2
Cooking Time: 12 Minutes
Ingredients:
- 8 ounces Chinese cabbage, roughly chopped
- 2 ounces bacon, chopped
- 1 tablespoon sunflower oil
- ½ teaspoon onion powder
- ½ teaspoon salt

Directions:
1. Cook the bacon at 400 degrees F/ 205 degrees C for almost 10 minutes.
2. Stir it from time to time. Then sprinkle it with onion powder and salt.
3. Add Chinese cabbage and shake the mixture well. Cook it for 2 minutes.
4. Then add sunflower oil, stir the meal and place in the serving plates.
5. Serve.

Kale And Brussels Sprouts

Servings: 8
Cooking Time: 15 Minutes
Ingredients:
- 1 pound Brussels sprouts, trimmed
- 2 cups kale, torn
- 1 tablespoon olive oil
- Black pepper and salt to the taste
- 3 ounces. mozzarella, shredded

Directions:
1. In a pan that fits the air fryer, combine all the recipe ingredients except the mozzarella and toss.
2. Put the pan in the preheated Air Fryer and Cook at almost 380 degrees F/ 195 degrees C for almost 15 minutes.
3. Divide between plates, sprinkle the cheese on top and serve.

Herb-roasted Vegetables

Servings: 4
Cooking Time: 14 To 18 Minutes
Ingredients:
- 1 red bell pepper, sliced
- 1 (8-ounce) package sliced mushrooms
- 1 cup green beans, cut into 2-inch pieces
- ⅓ cup diced red onion
- 3 garlic cloves, sliced
- 1 teaspoon olive oil (see Tip)
- ½ teaspoon dried basil
- ½ teaspoon dried tarragon

Directions:
1. In a medium bowl, mix the red bell pepper, mushrooms, green beans, red onion, and garlic. Drizzle with the olive oil. Toss to coat.
2. Add the herbs and toss again.
3. Place the vegetables in the air fryer basket. Roast for 14 to 18 minutes, or until tender. Serve immediately.

Air Fried Brussels Sprout

Servings: 1
Cooking Time: 10 Minutes
Ingredients:
- 1 pound (454 g) Brussels sprouts
- 1 tablespoon coconut oil, melted
- 1 tablespoon unsalted butter, melted

Directions:
1. Preheat the air fryer to 400°F (204°C).
2. Prepare the Brussels sprouts by halving them, discarding any loose leaves.
3. Combine with the melted coconut oil and transfer to the air fryer.
4. Air fry for 10 minutes, giving the basket a good shake throughout the air frying time to brown them up if desired.
5. The sprouts are ready when they are partially caramelized. Remove them from the air fryer and serve with a topping of melted butter before serving.

Tofu Bites

Servings: 4
Cooking Time: 30 Minutes
Ingredients:
- 1 packaged firm tofu, cubed and pressed to remove excess water
- 1 tablespoon soy sauce
- 1 tablespoon ketchup
- 1 tablespoon maple syrup
- ½ teaspoon vinegar
- 1 teaspoon liquid smoke
- 1 teaspoon hot sauce
- 2 tablespoons sesame seeds
- 1 teaspoon garlic powder
- Salt and ground black pepper, to taste
- Cooking spray

Directions:
1. Preheat the air fryer to 375°F (191°C).
2. Spritz a baking dish with cooking spray.
3. Combine all the ingredients to coat the tofu completely and allow the marinade to absorb for half an hour.
4. Transfer the tofu to the baking dish, then air fry for 15 minutes. Flip the tofu over and air fry for another 15 minutes on the other side.
5. Serve immediately.

Herbed Vegetable Mélange

Servings: 4
Cooking Time: 14 To 18 Minutes
Ingredients:
- 1 red bell pepper, sliced
- 1 (8-ounce) package sliced mushrooms
- 1 yellow summer squash, sliced
- 3 cloves garlic, sliced
- 1 tablespoon olive oil
- ½ teaspoon dried thyme
- ½ teaspoon dried basil
- ½ teaspoon dried tarragon

Directions:
1. Place the pepper, mushrooms, squash, and garlic in a medium bowl and drizzle with the olive oil. Toss, add the thyme, basil, and tarragon, and toss again.
2. Place the vegetables in the air fryer basket. Roast for 14 to 18 minutes or until the vegetables are tender.

Spicy Cauliflower Roast

Servings: 4
Cooking Time: 20 Minutes
Ingredients:
- Cauliflower:
- 5 cups cauliflower florets
- 3 tablespoons vegetable oil
- ½ teaspoon ground cumin
- ½ teaspoon ground coriander
- ½ teaspoon kosher salt
- Sauce:
- ½ cup Greek yogurt or sour cream
- ¼ cup chopped fresh cilantro
- 1 jalapeño, coarsely chopped
- 4 cloves garlic, peeled
- ½ teaspoon kosher salt
- 2 tablespoons water

Directions:
1. Preheat the air fryer to 400°F (204°C).
2. In a large bowl, combine the cauliflower, oil, cumin, coriander, and salt. Toss to coat.
3. Put the cauliflower in the air fryer basket. Roast for 20 minutes, stirring halfway through the roasting time.
4. Meanwhile, in a blender, combine the yogurt, cilantro, jalapeño, garlic, and salt. Blend, adding the water as needed to keep the blades moving and to thin the sauce.
5. At the end of roasting time, transfer the cauliflower to a large serving bowl. Pour the sauce over and toss gently to coat. Serve immediately.

Cashew Stuffed Mushrooms

Servings: 6
Cooking Time: 15 Minutes
Ingredients:
- 1 cup basil
- ½ cup cashew, soaked overnight
- ½ cup nutritional yeast
- 1 tablespoon lemon juice
- 2 cloves garlic
- 1 tablespoon olive oil
- Salt, to taste
- 1 pound (454 g) baby Bella mushroom, stems removed

Directions:
1. Preheat the air fryer to 400°F (204°C).
2. Prepare the pesto. In a food processor, blend the basil, cashew nuts, nutritional yeast, lemon juice, garlic and olive oil to combine well. Sprinkle with salt as desired.
3. Turn the mushrooms cap-side down and spread the pesto on the underside of each cap.
4. Transfer to the air fryer and air fry for 15 minutes.
5. Serve warm.

Cheese Spinach

Servings: 6
Cooking Time: 16 Minutes
Ingredients:
- 1-pound fresh spinach
- 6 ounces gouda cheese, shredded
- 8 ounces cream cheese
- 1 teaspoon garlic powder
- 1 tablespoon onion, minced
- Black pepper
- Salt

Directions:
1. At 370 degrees F/ 185 degrees C, preheat your air fryer.
2. Grease its air fryer basket with cooking spray and set aside.
3. Spray a large pan with cooking spray and heat over medium heat.
4. Add spinach to the same pan and cook until wilted.
5. Add cream cheese, garlic powder, and onion and stir until cheese is melted.
6. Remove pan from heat and add Gouda cheese and season with black pepper and salt.
7. Transfer spinach mixture to the prepared baking dish and place into the air fryer.
8. Cook for 16 minutes.
9. Serve and enjoy.

Mint Lemon Squash

Servings: 4
Cooking Time: 25 Minutes
Ingredients:
- 4 summer squash, cut into wedges
- ¼ cup olive oil
- ¼ cup lemon juice
- ½ cup mint, chopped
- 1 cup mozzarella, shredded
- Black pepper and salt to the taste

Directions:
1. In a suitable pan that fits your air fryer, mix the squash with the rest of the ingredients, toss, introduce the pan in the preheated air fryer and cook at almost 370 degrees F/ 185 degrees C for 25 minutes.
2. Serve.

Potato With Creamy Cheese

Servings: 2
Cooking Time: 15 Minutes
Ingredients:
- 2 medium potatoes
- 1 teaspoon butter
- 3 tablespoons sour cream
- 1 teaspoon chives
- 1½ tablespoons grated Parmesan cheese

Directions:
1. Preheat the air fryer to 350°F (177°C).
2. Pierce the potatoes with a fork and boil them in water until they are cooked.
3. Transfer to the air fryer and air fry for 15 minutes.
4. In the meantime, combine the sour cream, cheese and chives in a bowl. Cut the potatoes halfway to open them up and fill with the butter and sour cream mixture.
5. Serve immediately.

Scalloped Mixed Vegetables

Servings: 4
Cooking Time: 20 Minutes
Ingredients:
- 1 Yukon Gold potato, thinly sliced
- 1 small sweet potato, peeled and thinly sliced
- 1 medium carrot, thinly sliced
- ¼ cup minced onion
- 3 garlic cloves, minced
- ¾ cup 2 percent milk
- 2 tablespoons cornstarch
- ½ teaspoon dried thyme

Directions:
1. In a 6-by-2-inch pan, layer the potato, sweet potato, carrot, onion, and garlic.
2. In a small bowl, whisk the milk, cornstarch, and thyme until blended. Pour the milk mixture evenly over the vegetables in the pan.
3. Bake for 15 minutes. Check the casserole—it should be golden brown on top, and the vegetables should be tender. If they aren't, bake for 4 to 5 minutes more. Serve immediately.

Sweet Potatoes With Zucchini

Servings: 4
Cooking Time: 20 Minutes
Ingredients:
- 2 large-sized sweet potatoes, peeled and quartered
- 1 medium zucchini, sliced
- 1 Serrano pepper, deseeded and thinly sliced
- 1 bell pepper, deseeded and thinly sliced
- 1 to 2 carrots, cut into matchsticks
- ¼ cup olive oil
- 1½ tablespoons maple syrup
- ½ teaspoon porcini powder
- ¼ teaspoon mustard powder
- ½ teaspoon fennel seeds
- 1 tablespoon garlic powder
- ½ teaspoon fine sea salt
- ¼ teaspoon ground black pepper
- Tomato ketchup, for serving

Directions:
1. Put the sweet potatoes, zucchini, peppers, and the carrot into the air fryer basket. Coat with a drizzling of olive oil.
2. Preheat the air fryer to 350°F (177°C).
3. Air fry the vegetables for 15 minutes.
4. In the meantime, prepare the sauce by vigorously combining the other ingredients, except for the tomato ketchup, with a whisk.
5. Lightly grease a baking dish.
6. Transfer the cooked vegetables to the baking dish, pour over the sauce and coat the vegetables well.
7. Increase the temperature to 390°F (199°C) and air fry the vegetables for an additional 5 minutes.
8. Serve warm with a side of ketchup.

Cheese Broccoli With Basil

Servings: 4
Cooking Time: 7 Minutes
Ingredients:
- 1 cup broccoli, chopped, boiled
- 1 teaspoon nut oil
- 1 teaspoon salt
- 1 teaspoon dried basil
- ½ cup Cheddar cheese, shredded
- ½ cup of coconut milk
- ½ teaspoon butter, softened

Directions:
1. In the air fryer basket, place the broccoli, nut oil, dried dill, and salt.
2. Stir together the mixture and then pour in the coconut milk.
3. Drizzle butter and Cheddar cheese on the top of the meal.
4. Before cooking, heat your air fryer to 400 degrees F/ 205 degrees C.
5. Cook the mixture inside the preheated air fryer for 7 minutes.

Fried Brussel Sprouts

Servings: 4
Cooking Time: 20 Minutes
Ingredients:
- 1 pound Brussels sprouts, trimmed and halved
- Salt and black pepper to the taste
- 2 tablespoons ghee, melted
- ½ cup coconut cream
- 2 tablespoons garlic, minced
- 1 tablespoon chives, chopped

Directions:
1. Grease the air fryer basket with the melted ghee.
2. Mix the Brussels sprouts with the remaining ingredients in the air fryer basket.
3. Cook in your air fryer at 370 degrees F/ 185 degrees C for 20 minutes.
4. Serve on plates as a side dish.

Portobello Pizzas

Servings: 4
Cooking Time: 10 Minutes
Ingredients:
- Olive oil
- 4 large portobello mushroom caps, cleaned and stems removed
- Garlic powder
- 8 tablespoons pizza sauce
- 16 slices turkey pepperoni
- 8 tablespoons mozzarella cheese

Directions:
1. Spray a fryer basket lightly with olive oil.
2. Lightly spray the outside of the mushrooms with olive oil and sprinkle with a little garlic powder, to taste.
3. Turn the mushroom over and lightly spray the sides and top edges of the mushroom with olive oil and sprinkle with garlic powder, to taste.
4. Place the mushrooms in the fryer basket in a single layer with the top side down. Leave room between the mushrooms. You may need to cook them in batches.
5. Air fry for 5 minutes.
6. Spoon 2 tablespoons of pizza sauce on each mushroom. Top each with 4 slices of turkey pepperoni and sprinkle with 2 tablespoons of mozzarella cheese. Press the pepperoni and cheese down into the pizza sauce to help prevent it from flying around inside the air fryer.
7. Air fry until the cheese is melted and lightly browned on top, another 3 to 5 minutes.

Crispy Chickpeas

Servings:4
Cooking Time: 15 Minutes
Ingredients:
- 1 (15-ounces / 425-g) can chickpeas, drained but not rinsed
- 2 tablespoons olive oil
- 1 teaspoon salt
- 2 tablespoons lemon juice

Directions:
1. Preheat the air fryer to 400°F (204°C).
2. Add all the ingredients together in a bowl and mix. Transfer this mixture to the air fryer basket.
3. Air fry for 15 minutes, ensuring the chickpeas become nice and crispy.
4. Serve immediately.

Basmati Risotto

Servings: 2
Cooking Time: 30 Minutes
Ingredients:
- 1 onion, diced
- 1 small carrot, diced
- 2 cups vegetable broth, boiling
- ½ cup grated Cheddar cheese
- 1 clove garlic, minced
- ¾ cup long-grain basmati rice
- 1 tablespoon olive oil
- 1 tablespoon unsalted butter

Directions:
1. Preheat the air fryer to 390°F (199°C).
2. Grease a baking tin with oil and stir in the butter, garlic, carrot, and onion.
3. Put the tin in the air fryer and bake for 4 minutes.
4. Pour in the rice and bake for a further 4 minutes, stirring three times throughout the baking time.
5. Turn the temperature down to 320°F (160°C).
6. Add the vegetable broth and give the dish a gentle stir. Bake for 22 minutes, leaving the air fryer uncovered.
7. Pour in the cheese, stir once more and serve.

Crispy Brussels Sprouts

Servings: 4
Cooking Time: 15 Minutes
Ingredients:
- For the Brussels sprouts
- 1 pound Brussels sprouts, halved (2 cups)
- 1 teaspoon garlic powder
- Salt
- Pepper
- Cooking oil
- For the mustard aioli
- ½ cup mayonnaise
- ½ tablespoon olive oil
- 1 tablespoon Dijon mustard
- 1 teaspoon minced garlic
- Salt
- Pepper
- 1 tablespoon chopped parsley

Directions:
1. In a large bowl, combine the Brussels sprouts with the garlic powder. Season with salt and pepper to taste.
2. Place the Brussels sprouts in the air fryer. Spray them with cooking oil. Cook for 6 minutes.
3. Open the air fryer and shake the basket. Cook for an additional 6 to 7 minutes, until the Brussels sprouts have turned slightly brown.
4. While the Brussels sprouts are cooking, combine the mayonnaise, olive oil, mustard, and garlic in a small bowl, adding salt and pepper to taste. Mix well until fully combined. Sprinkle with parsley to garnish.
5. Cool the Brussels sprouts and serve alongside the aioli.

Mascarpone Mushrooms

Servings: 4
Cooking Time: 15 Minutes
Ingredients:
- Vegetable oil spray
- 4 cups sliced mushrooms
- 1 medium yellow onion, chopped
- 2 cloves garlic, minced
- ¼ cup heavy whipping cream or half-and-half
- 8 ounces (227 g) mascarpone cheese
- 1 teaspoon dried thyme
- 1 teaspoon kosher salt
- 1 teaspoon black pepper
- ½ teaspoon red pepper flakes
- 4 cups cooked konjac noodles, for serving
- ½ cup grated Parmesan cheese

Directions:
1. Preheat the air fryer to 350°F (177°C). Spray a heatproof pan with vegetable oil spray.
2. In a medium bowl, combine the mushrooms, onion, garlic, cream, mascarpone, thyme, salt, black pepper, and red pepper flakes. Stir to combine. Transfer the mixture to the prepared pan.
3. Put the pan in the air fryer basket. Bake for 15 minutes, stirring halfway through the baking time.
4. Divide the pasta among four shallow bowls. Spoon the mushroom mixture evenly over the pasta. Sprinkle with Parmesan cheese and serve.

Savory Roasted Sweet Potatoes

Servings: 4
Cooking Time: 25 Minutes
Ingredients:
- 2 sweet potatoes, peeled and cut into 1-inch cubes
- 1 tablespoon olive oil
- Pinch salt
- Freshly ground black pepper
- ½ teaspoon dried thyme
- ½ teaspoon dried marjoram
- ¼ cup grated Parmesan cheese

Directions:
1. Put the sweet potato cubes in the air fryer basket and drizzle with the olive oil. Toss gently. Sprinkle with the salt, pepper, thyme, and marjoram, and toss again.
2. Roast for 20 minutes, shaking the air fryer basket once during cooking time.
3. Remove the basket from the air fryer and shake the potatoes again. Sprinkle evenly with the Parmesan cheese and return to the air fryer.
4. Roast for 5 minutes or until the potatoes are tender.
5. Did You Know? Sweet potatoes and yams are two different types of root vegetable. A true yam is a starchy white root vegetable used in Caribbean cooking. Sweet potatoes are high in vitamin A and are usually bright orange in color.

Garlic And Sesame Carrots

Servings: 6
Cooking Time: 16 Minutes
Ingredients:
- 1 pound baby carrots
- 1 tablespoon sesame oil
- ½ teaspoon dried dill
- Pinch salt
- Freshly ground black pepper
- 6 cloves garlic, peeled
- 3 tablespoons sesame seeds

Directions:
1. Place the baby carrots in a medium bowl. Drizzle with sesame oil, add the dill, salt, and pepper, and toss to coat well.
2. Place the carrots in the basket of the air fryer. Roast for 8 minutes, shaking the basket once during cooking time.
3. Add the garlic to the air fryer. Roast for 8 minutes, shaking the basket once during cooking time, or until the garlic and carrots are lightly browned.
4. Transfer to a serving bowl and sprinkle with the sesame seeds before serving.

Buttered Kale Mix

Servings: 2
Cooking Time: 12 Minutes
Ingredients:
- 3 tablespoons butter, melted
- 2 cups kale leaves
- Black pepper and salt to taste
- ½ cup yellow onion, chopped
- 2 teaspoons turmeric powder

Directions:
1. Place all the recipe ingredients in a pan that fits your air fryer and mix well.
2. Put the pan in the air fryer and cook at almost 250 degrees F/ 120 degrees C for 12 minutes.
3. Divide between plates and serve.

Kidney Beans Oatmeal In Peppers

Servings: 4
Cooking Time: 6 Minutes
Ingredients:
- 2 large bell peppers, halved lengthwise, deseeded
- 2 tablespoons cooked kidney beans
- 2 tablespoons cooked chick peas
- 2 cups cooked oatmeal
- 1 teaspoon ground cumin
- ½ teaspoon paprika
- ½ teaspoon salt or to taste
- ¼ teaspoon black pepper powder
- ¼ cup yogurt

Directions:
1. Preheat the air fryer to 355°F (179°C).
2. Put the bell peppers, cut-side down, in the air fryer basket. Air fry for 2 minutes.
3. Take the peppers out of the air fryer and let cool.
4. In a bowl, combine the rest of the ingredients.
5. Divide the mixture evenly and use each portion to stuff a pepper.
6. Return the stuffed peppers to the air fryer and continue to air fry for 4 minutes.
7. Serve hot.

Roasted Brussels Sprouts

Servings: 4
Cooking Time: 20 Minutes
Ingredients:
- 1 pound fresh Brussels sprouts
- 1 tablespoon olive oil
- ½ teaspoon salt
- ⅛ teaspoon pepper
- ¼ cup grated Parmesan cheese

Directions:
1. Trim the bottoms from the Brussels sprouts and pull off any discolored leaves. Toss with the olive oil, salt, and pepper, and place in the air fryer basket.
2. Roast for 20 minutes, shaking the air fryer basket twice during cooking time, until the Brussels sprouts are dark golden brown and crisp.
3. Transfer the Brussels sprouts to a serving dish and toss with the Parmesan cheese. Serve immediately.
4. Did You Know? Brussels sprouts were cultivated in Roman times and introduced into the United States in the 1880s. Most Brussels sprouts in this country are grown in California.

Gorgonzola Mushrooms With Horseradish Mayo

Servings: 5
Cooking Time: 10 Minutes
Ingredients:
- ½ cup bread crumbs
- 2 cloves garlic, pressed
- 2 tablespoons chopped fresh coriander
- ⅓ teaspoon kosher salt
- ½ teaspoon crushed red pepper flakes
- 1½ tablespoons olive oil
- 20 medium mushrooms, stems removed
- ½ cup grated Gorgonzola cheese
- ¼ cup low-fat mayonnaise
- 1 teaspoon prepared horseradish, well-drained
- 1 tablespoon finely chopped fresh parsley

Directions:
1. Preheat the air fryer to 380°F (193°C).
2. Combine the bread crumbs together with the garlic, coriander, salt, red pepper, and olive oil.
3. Take equal-sized amounts of the breadcrumb mixture and use them to stuff the mushroom caps. Add the grated Gorgonzola on top of each.
4. Put the mushrooms in the air fryer baking pan and transfer to the air fryer.
5. Air fry for 10 minutes, ensuring the stuffing is warm throughout.
6. In the meantime, prepare the horseradish mayo. Mix the mayonnaise, horseradish and parsley.
7. When the mushrooms are ready, serve with the mayo.

Mashed Chives And Celery

Servings: 4
Cooking Time: 20 Minutes
Ingredients:
- 14 ounces celery stalks
- 1 cup cauliflower florets
- Black pepper and salt to the taste
- 2 garlic cloves, minced
- ⅓ cup heavy cream
- 4 ounces butter, melted
- 1 tablespoon chives, chopped
- Zest of 1 lemon, grated

Directions:
1. Mix all the recipe ingredients except the chives and the cream in a suitable pan.
2. Introduce this pan to the air fryer and air fryer at almost 360 degrees F/ 180 degrees C for 20 minutes.
3. Mash the mix, add the rest of the ingredients, whisk well.
4. Serve.

Broccoli With Paprika

Servings: 4
Cooking Time: 15 Minutes
Ingredients:
- 1 broccoli head, florets separated
- Black pepper and salt to the taste
- ½ cup keto tomato sauce
- 1 tablespoon sweet paprika
- ¼ cup scallions, chopped
- 1 tablespoon olive oil

Directions:
1. In a pan that fits the air fryer, combine the broccoli with the rest of the ingredients, toss, put the pan in the air fryer and cook at almost 380 degrees F/ 195 degrees C for almost 15 minutes.
2. Divide between plates and serve.

Black Bean And Tomato Chili

Servings: 6
Cooking Time: 23 Minutes
Ingredients:
- 1 tablespoon olive oil
- 1 medium onion, diced
- 3 garlic cloves, minced
- 1 cup vegetable broth
- 3 cans black beans, drained and rinsed
- 2 cans diced tomatoes
- 2 chipotle peppers, chopped
- 2 teaspoons cumin
- 2 teaspoons chili powder
- 1 teaspoon dried oregano
- ½ teaspoon salt

Directions:
1. Over a medium heat, fry the garlic and onions in the olive oil for 3 minutes.
2. Add the remaining ingredients, stirring constantly and scraping the bottom to prevent sticking.
3. Preheat the air fryer to 400°F (204°C).
4. Take a dish and place the mixture inside. Put a sheet of aluminum foil on top.
5. Transfer to the air fryer and bake for 20 minutes.
6. When ready, plate up and serve immediately.

Mozzarella Veggie Tacos

Servings: 3
Cooking Time: 30 Minutes
Ingredients:
- 1 cup kidney beans, drained
- 1 cup black beans, drained
- ½ cup tomato puree
- 1 fresh jalapeño chili, chopped
- 1 cup fresh cilantro, chopped
- 1 cup corn kernels
- ½ teaspoon ground cumin
- ½ teaspoon cayenne pepper
- Salt and black pepper
- 1 cup grated mozzarella cheese
- Guacamole to serve

Directions:
1. Add kidney beans, black beans, tomato puree, jalapeno chili, the chopped cilantro, corn, ground cumin, cayenne pepper, salt, and pepper in a mixing bowl. Stir together.
2. Spoon the mixture onto the half of the taco.
3. Sprinkle the top with the mozzarella cheese and fold.
4. Spray the air fryer basket with cooking spray.
5. Ladle the tacos inside the air fryer basket.
6. Then cook in your air fryer at 360 degrees F/ 180 degrees C for 14 minutes.
7. When cooked, remove from the air fryer and serve hot with guacamole.

Roasted Spiced Broccoli With Masala

Servings: 2
Cooking Time: 15 Minutes
Ingredients:
- ¼ teaspoon chat masala
- ¼ teaspoon turmeric powder
- ½ teaspoon salt
- 1 tablespoon chickpea flour
- 2 cups broccoli florets
- 2 tablespoons yogurt

Directions:
1. In a bowl, add chat masala, turmeric powder, salt, chickpea flour, broccoli florets, and yogurt and combine together.
2. Transfer the mixture inside the air fryer baking pan.
3. Cook in your air fryer at 330 degrees F/ 165 degrees C for 15 minutes.
4. Halfway through cooking, shake the baking pan.

Herbed Potatoes With Tomato Sauce

Servings: 4
Cooking Time: 16 Minutes
Ingredients:
- 2 pounds potatoes; cubed
- 4 garlic cloves; minced
- 1 yellow onion; chopped.
- 1 cup tomato sauce
- ½ teaspoon oregano; dried
- ½ teaspoon parsley; dried
- 2 tablespoons basil; chopped
- 2 tablespoons olive oil

Directions:
1. Heat up a pan that fits your air fryer with the oil over medium heat, add onion; stir and cook for 1-2 minutes.
2. Add garlic, potatoes, parsley, tomato sauce and oregano; stir, introduce in your air fryer and cook at almost 370 degrees F/ 185 degrees C and cook for 16 minutes.
3. Add basil, toss everything, divide among plates and serve.

Creamy Cauliflower Mash

Servings: 4
Cooking Time: 20 Minutes
Ingredients:
- 2 pounds cauliflower florets
- 1 teaspoon olive oil
- 2 ounces parmesan, grated
- 4 ounces butter, soft
- Juice of ½ lemon
- Zest of ½ lemon, grated
- Salt and black pepper to the taste

Directions:
1. Before cooking, heat your air fryer with the air fryer basket to 380 degrees F/ 195 degrees C.
2. Add the cauliflower in the preheated air fryer basket and add oil to rub well.
3. Cook in your air fryer for 20 minutes.
4. When cooked, remove the cauliflower to a bowl. Mash well and place the remaining ingredients in the bowl. Stir well.
5. Serve on plates as a side dish.

Herbed Radishes

Servings: 2
Cooking Time: 10 Minutes
Ingredients:
- 1 pound (454 g) radishes
- 2 tablespoons unsalted butter, melted
- ¼ teaspoon dried oregano
- ½ teaspoon dried parsley
- ½ teaspoon garlic powder

Directions:
1. Preheat the air fryer to 350°F (177°C). Prepare the radishes by cutting off their tops and bottoms and quartering them.
2. In a bowl, combine the butter, dried oregano, dried parsley, and garlic powder. Toss with the radishes to coat.
3. Transfer the radishes to the air fryer and air fry for 10 minutes, shaking the basket at the halfway point to ensure the radishes air fry evenly through. The radishes are ready when they turn brown.
4. Serve immediately.

Air Fried Potatoes With Olives

Servings: 1
Cooking Time: 40 Minutes
Ingredients:
- 1 medium russet potato, scrubbed and peeled
- 1 teaspoon olive oil
- ¼ teaspoon onion powder
- ⅛ teaspoon salt
- Dollop of butter
- Dollop of cream cheese
- 1 tablespoon Kalamata olives
- 1 tablespoon chopped chives

Directions:
1. Preheat the air fryer to 400°F (204°C).
2. In a bowl, coat the potatoes with the onion powder, salt, olive oil, and butter.
3. Transfer to the air fryer and air fry for 40 minutes, turning the potatoes over at the halfway point.
4. Take care when removing the potatoes from the air fryer and serve with the cream cheese, Kalamata olives and chives on top.

Lemon Fennel With Sunflower Seeds

Servings: 4
Cooking Time: 15 Minutes
Ingredients:
- 1 pound fennel, cut into small wedges
- A pinch of salt and black pepper
- 3 tablespoons olive oil
- Salt and black pepper to the taste
- Juice of ½ lemon
- 2 tablespoons sunflower seeds

Directions:
1. Mix fennel wedges, salt, black pepper, olive oil, and lemon in a suitable baking pan.
2. Cook the mixture in your air fryer at 400 degrees F/ 205 degrees C for 15 minutes.
3. When cooked, sprinkle on top with the sunflower seeds.
4. Serve on plates as a side dish.

Broccoli Cheese Tots

Servings: 4
Cooking Time: 15 Minutes
Ingredients:
- Olive oil
- 12 ounces frozen broccoli, thawed and drained
- 1 large egg
- 1½ teaspoons minced garlic
- ¼ cup grated Parmesan cheese
- ¼ cup shredded reduced-fat sharp Cheddar cheese
- ½ cup seasoned whole-wheat bread crumbs
- Salt
- Freshly ground black pepper

Directions:
1. Spray the fryer basket lightly with olive oil.
2. Gently squeeze the thawed broccoli to remove any excess liquid.
3. In a food processor, combine the broccoli, egg, garlic, Parmesan cheese, Cheddar cheese, bread crumbs, salt, and pepper and pulse until it resembles a coarse meal.
4. Using a tablespoon, scoop up the broccoli mixture and shape into 24 oval "tater tot" shapes.
5. Place the tots in the fryer basket in a single layer, being careful to space them a little bit apart. Lightly spray the tots with oil. You may need to cook them in batches.
6. Air fry for 6 to 7 minutes. Turn the tots over and cook for an additional 6 to 8 minutes or until lightly browned and crispy.

Roasted Bell Peppers With Garlic

Servings: 4
Cooking Time: 22 Minutes
Ingredients:
- 1 red bell pepper
- 1 yellow bell pepper
- 1 orange bell pepper
- 1 green bell pepper
- 2 tablespoons olive oil, divided
- ½ teaspoon dried marjoram
- Pinch salt
- Freshly ground black pepper
- 1 head garlic

Directions:
1. Slice the bell peppers into 1-inch strips.
2. In a large bowl, toss the bell peppers with 1 tablespoon of the oil. Sprinkle on the marjoram, salt, and pepper, and toss again.
3. Cut off the top of the garlic head and place the cloves on an oiled square of aluminum foil. Drizzle with the remaining olive oil. Wrap the garlic in the foil.
4. Place the wrapped garlic in the air fryer and roast for 15 minutes, then add the bell peppers. Roast for 7 minutes or until the peppers are tender and the garlic is soft. Transfer the peppers to a serving dish.
5. Remove the garlic from the air fryer and unwrap the foil. When cool enough to handle, squeeze the garlic cloves out of the papery skin and mix with the bell peppers.

Poultry Recipes

Dijon Chicken Breasts

Servings: 6
Cooking Time: 24 Minutes
Ingredients:
- 6 (6-oz, each) Boneless, skinless chicken breasts
- 2 tablespoons Fresh rosemary, minced
- 3 tablespoons Honey
- 1 tablespoon Dijon mustard
- Black pepper and salt to taste

Directions:
1. Combine the mustard, honey, black pepper, rosemary and salt in a suitable bowl. Rub the chicken with this mixture.
2. Grease its air fryer basket with oil.
3. Air fry the chicken at 350 degrees F/ 175 degrees C for 20 to 24 minutes or until the chicken' inner doneness reaches 165 degrees F/ 75 degrees C.
4. Serve.

Orange Chicken

Servings: 2 Servings
Cooking Time: 20 Minutes
Ingredients:
- 1 pound of chopped chicken breast
- 2 tablespoons of cornstarch + 2 teaspoons for the sauce
- ½ cup of orange juice
- 2 tablespoons of sugar
- 1 tablespoon of vinegar
- 1 tablespoon of soy sauce
- ¼ teaspoon of ground ginger
- Zest of 1 orange
- Dash of red pepper flakes
- Pinch of salt and black pepper, to taste

Directions:
1. Preheat your air fryer to 400°F.
2. Add chicken pieces with 2 tablespoons of cornstarch in a bowl and mix well until they are fully coated. Cook them in the air fryer at 400°F for 7–9 minutes. Toss halfway through cooking.
3. Meanwhile, mix sugar, orange juice, soy sauce, vinegar, red pepper flakes, orange zest, and ginger in a small saucepan. Put on medium heat and simmer for 5 minutes.
4. Combine 2 teaspoons of cornstarch with 2 teaspoons of water in a small bowl. Pour the prepared mixture into the orange sauce. Continue simmering for 1 more minute. Remove from the heat.
5. Take the cooked chicken from the air fryer and mix it with sauce.
6. Serve warm* and enjoy your Orange Chicken!

Bacon-wrapped Chicken

Servings: 14 Bites
Cooking Time: 30 Minutes
Ingredients:
- 2 skinless chicken breasts
- 7 slices of uncooked bacon
- 1 cup of barbecue sauce
- 2 tablespoons of brown sugar

Directions:
1. Preheat your air fryer to 400°F. Spray the air fryer basket with some oil.
2. Cut each breast into 7 equal strips, so in total you will have 14 sticks at the end. Slice each bacon piece in half lengthwise.
3. Wrap each chicken piece with the bacon slice. Brush the top with the barbecue sauce and sprinkle some brown sugar over it.
4. Put the prepared chicken in the preheated air fryer basket and cook at 400°F for 5 minutes. Flip it and continue cooking for 5 minutes. If chicken is not 165°F internally, cook for additional 3–5 minutes.
5. Serve* warm and enjoy your Bacon-Wrapped Chicken!

Warm Chicken And Spinach Salad

Servings: 4
Cooking Time: 16 To 20 Minutes
Ingredients:
- 3 (5-ounce) low-sodium boneless skinless chicken breasts, cut into 1-inch cubes
- 5 teaspoons olive oil
- ½ teaspoon dried thyme
- 1 medium red onion, sliced
- 1 red bell pepper, sliced
- 1 small zucchini, cut into strips
- 3 tablespoons freshly squeezed lemon juice
- 6 cups fresh baby spinach (see Tip)

Directions:
1. In a large bowl, mix the chicken with the olive oil and thyme. Toss to coat. Transfer to a medium metal bowl and roast for 8 minutes in the air fryer.
2. Add the red onion, red bell pepper, and zucchini. Roast for 8 to 12 minutes more, stirring once during cooking, or until the chicken reaches an internal temperature of 165°F on a meat thermometer.
3. Remove the bowl from the air fryer and stir in the lemon juice.
4. Put the spinach in a serving bowl and top with the chicken mixture. Toss to combine and serve immediately.

Spicy Coconut Chicken Wings

Servings: 4
Cooking Time: 20 Minutes
Ingredients:
- For the coconut chicken
- 16 chicken drumettes (party wings)
- ¼ cup full-fat coconut milk
- 1 tablespoon Sriracha
- 1 teaspoon onion powder
- 1 teaspoon garlic powder
- Salt
- Pepper
- ⅓ cup shredded unsweetened coconut
- ½ cup all-purpose flour
- Cooking oil
- For the mango salsa
- 1 cup mango sliced into ½ inch chunks
- ¼ cup cilantro, chopped
- ½ cup red onion, chopped
- 2 garlic cloves, minced
- Juice of ½ lime

Directions:
1. Place the drumettes in a sealable plastic bag.
2. In a small bowl, combine the coconut milk and Sriracha. Whisk until fully combined.
3. Drizzle the drumettes with the spicy coconut milk mixture. Season the drumettes with the onion powder, garlic powder, and salt and pepper to taste.
4. Seal the bag. Shake it thoroughly to combine the seasonings and coat the chicken. Marinate for at least 30 minutes, preferably overnight, in the refrigerator.
5. When the drumettes are almost done marinating, combine the shredded coconut and flour in a large bowl. Stir.
6. Spray the air fryer basket with cooking oil.
7. Dip the drumettes in the coconut and flour mixture. Place the drumettes in the air fryer. It is okay to stack them on top of each other. Spray the drumettes with cooking oil, being sure to cover the bottom layer. Cook for 5 minutes.
8. Remove the basket and shake it to ensure all of the pieces will cook fully.
9. Return the basket to the air fryer and continue to cook the chicken. Repeat shaking every 5 minutes until a total of 20 minutes has passed.
10. Cool before serving.

Whole Roasted Chicken

Servings: 6
Cooking Time: 1 Hour
Ingredients:
- Olive oil
- 1 teaspoon salt
- 1 teaspoon Italian seasoning
- ½ teaspoon freshly ground black pepper
- ½ teaspoon paprika
- ½ teaspoon garlic powder
- ½ teaspoon onion powder
- 2 tablespoons olive oil
- 1 (4-pound) fryer chicken

Directions:
1. Spray a fryer basket lightly with olive oil.
2. In a small bowl, mix together the salt, Italian seasoning, pepper, paprika, garlic powder, and onion powder.
3. Remove any giblets from the chicken. Pat the chicken dry very thoroughly with paper towels, including the cavity.
4. Brush the chicken all over with the olive oil and rub it with the seasoning mixture.
5. Truss the chicken or tie the legs with butcher's twine. This will make it easier to flip the chicken during cooking.
6. Place the chicken in the fryer basket, breast side down. Air fry for 30 minutes. Flip the chicken over and baste it with any drippings collected in the bottom drawer of the air fryer. Lightly spray the chicken with olive oil.
7. Air fry for 20 minutes. Flip the chicken over one last time and cook until a thermometer inserted into the thickest part of the thigh reaches at least 165°F and it's crispy and golden, 10 more minutes. Continue to cook, checking every 5 minutes until the chicken reaches the correct internal temperature.
8. Let the chicken rest for 10 minutes before carving.

Stir-fried Chicken With Mixed Fruit

Servings: 4
Cooking Time:14 To 15 Minutes
Ingredients:
- 1 pound low-sodium boneless skinless chicken breasts, cut into 1-inch pieces
- 1 medium red onion, chopped
- 1 (8-ounce) can pineapple chunks, drained, ¼ cup juice reserved
- 1 tablespoon peanut oil or safflower oil
- 1 peach, peeled, pitted, and cubed
- 1 tablespoon cornstarch
- ½ teaspoon ground ginger
- ¼ teaspoon ground allspice
- Brown rice, cooked (optional)

Directions:
1. In a medium metal bowl, mix the chicken, red onion, pineapple, and peanut oil. Cook in the air fryer for 9 minutes. Remove and stir.
2. Add the peach and return the bowl to the air fryer. Cook for 3 minutes more. Remove and stir again.
3. In a small bowl, whisk the reserved pineapple juice, the cornstarch, ginger, and allspice well. Add to the chicken mixture and stir to combine.
4. Cook for 2 to 3 minutes more, or until the chicken reaches an internal temperature of 165°F on a meat thermometer and the sauce is slightly thickened.
5. Serve immediately over hot cooked brown rice, if desired.

Turkish Chicken Kebabs

Servings:4
Cooking Time: 15 Minutes
Ingredients:
- ¼ cup plain Greek yogurt
- 1 tablespoon minced garlic
- 1 tablespoon tomato paste
- 1 tablespoon fresh lemon juice
- 1 tablespoon vegetable oil
- 1 teaspoon kosher salt
- 1 teaspoon ground cumin
- 1 teaspoon sweet Hungarian paprika
- ½ teaspoon ground cinnamon
- ½ teaspoon black pepper
- ½ teaspoon cayenne pepper
- 1 pound (454 g) boneless, skinless chicken thighs, quartered crosswise

Directions:
1. In a large bowl, combine the yogurt, garlic, tomato paste, lemon juice, vegetable oil, salt, cumin, paprika, cinnamon, black pepper, and cayenne. Stir until the spices are blended into the yogurt.
2. Add the chicken to the bowl and toss until well coated. Marinate at room temperature for 30 minutes, or cover and refrigerate for up to 24 hours.
3. Preheat the air fryer to 375°F (191°C).
4. Arrange the chicken in a single layer in the air fryer basket. Air fry for 10 minutes. Turn the chicken and air fry for 5 minutes more. Use a meat thermometer to ensure the chicken has reached an internal temperature of 165°F (74°C).
5. Serve warm.

Garlic Soy Chicken Thighs

Servings:2
Cooking Time: 30 Minutes
Ingredients:
- 2 tablespoons chicken stock
- 2 tablespoons reduced-sodium soy sauce
- 1½ tablespoons sugar
- 4 garlic cloves, smashed and peeled
- 2 large scallions, cut into 2- to 3-inch batons, plus more, thinly sliced, for garnish
- 2 bone-in, skin-on chicken thighs (7 to 8 ounces / 198 to 227 g each)

Directions:
1. Preheat the air fryer to 375°F (191°C).
2. In a metal cake pan, combine the chicken stock, soy sauce, and sugar and stir until the sugar dissolves. Add the garlic cloves, scallions, and chicken thighs, turning the thighs to coat them in the marinade, then resting them skin-side up. Place the pan in the air fryer and bake, flipping the thighs every 5 minutes after the first 10 minutes, until the chicken is cooked through and the marinade is reduced to a sticky glaze over the chicken, about 30 minutes.
3. Remove the pan from the air fryer and serve the chicken thighs warm, with any remaining glaze spooned over top and sprinkled with more sliced scallions.

Buffalo Chicken Taquitos

Servings: 6
Cooking Time: 10 Minutes
Ingredients:
- Olive oil
- 8 ounces fat-free cream cheese, softened
- ⅛ cup Buffalo sauce
- 2 cups shredded cooked chicken
- 12 (7-inch) low-carb flour tortillas

Directions:
1. Spray a fryer basket lightly with olive oil.
2. In a large bowl, mix together the cream cheese and Buffalo sauce until well-combined. Add the chicken and stir until combined.
3. Place the tortillas on a clean workspace. Spoon 2 to 3 tablespoons of the chicken mixture in a thin line down the center of each tortilla. Roll up the tortillas.
4. Place the tortillas in the fryer basket, seam side down. Spray each tortilla lightly with olive oil. You may need to cook the taquitos in batches.
5. Air fry until golden brown, 5 to 10 minutes.

Air Fryer Naked Chicken Tenders

Servings: 4
Cooking Time: 7 Minutes
Ingredients:
- Seasoning:
- 1 teaspoon kosher salt
- ½ teaspoon garlic powder
- ½ teaspoon onion powder
- ½ teaspoon chili powder
- ¼ teaspoon sweet paprika
- ¼ teaspoon freshly ground black pepper
- Chicken:
- 8 chicken breast tenders (1 pound / 454 g total)
- 2 tablespoons mayonnaise

Directions:
1. Preheat the air fryer to 375°F (191°C).
2. For the seasoning: In a small bowl, combine the salt, garlic powder, onion powder, chili powder, paprika, and pepper.
3. For the chicken: Place the chicken in a medium bowl and add the mayonnaise. Mix well to coat all over, then sprinkle with the seasoning mix.
4. Working in batches, arrange a single layer of the chicken in the air fryer basket. Air fry for 6 to 7 minutes, flipping halfway, until cooked through in the center. Serve immediately.

Buttermilk Country-fried Chicken Wings

Servings: 4
Cooking Time: 20 Minutes
Ingredients:
- 16 chicken drumettes (party wings)
- 1 teaspoon garlic powder
- Chicken seasoning or rub
- Pepper
- ½ cup all-purpose flour
- ¼ cup low-fat buttermilk
- Cooking oil

Directions:
1. Place the chicken in a sealable plastic bag. Add the garlic powder, then add chicken seasoning or rub and pepper to taste. Seal the bag. Shake the bag thoroughly to combine the seasonings and coat the chicken.
2. Pour the flour into a second sealable plastic bag.
3. Pour the buttermilk into a bowl large enough to dunk the chicken. One at a time, dunk the drumettes in the buttermilk, then place them in the bag of flour. Seal and shake to thoroughly coat the chicken.
4. Spray the air fryer basket with cooking oil.
5. Using tongs, transfer the chicken from the bag to the air fryer basket. It is okay to stack the drumettes on top of each other. Spray the chicken with cooking oil, being sure to cover the bottom layer. Cook for 5 minutes.
6. Remove the basket and shake it to ensure all of the chicken pieces will cook fully.
7. Return the basket to the air fryer and continue to cook the chicken. Repeat shaking every 5 minutes until 20 minutes has passed.
8. Cool before serving.

Yellow Curry Chicken Thighs With Peanuts

Servings: 6
Cooking Time: 20 Minutes
Ingredients:
- ½ cup unsweetened full-fat coconut milk
- 2 tablespoons yellow curry paste
- 1 tablespoon minced fresh ginger
- 1 tablespoon minced garlic
- 1 teaspoon kosher salt
- 1 pound (454 g) boneless, skinless chicken thighs, halved crosswise
- 2 tablespoons chopped peanuts

Directions:
1. In a large bowl, stir together the coconut milk, curry paste, ginger, garlic, and salt until well blended. Add the chicken; toss well to coat. Marinate at room temperature for 30 minutes, or cover and refrigerate for up to 24 hours.
2. Preheat the air fryer to 375°F (191°C).
3. Place the chicken (along with marinade) in a baking pan. Place the pan in the air fryer basket. Bake for 20 minutes, turning the chicken halfway through the cooking time. Use a meat thermometer to ensure the chicken has reached an internal temperature of 165°F (74°C).
4. Sprinkle the chicken with the chopped peanuts and serve.

Classical Greek Keftedes

Servings: 2
Cooking Time: 10 Minutes
Ingredients:
- ½ pound ground chicken
- 1 egg
- 1 slice stale bread, cubed and soaked in milk
- 1 teaspoon fresh garlic, pressed
- 2 tablespoons Romano cheese, grated
- 1 bell pepper, deveined and chopped
- 1 teaspoon olive oil
- ½ teaspoon dried oregano
- ½ teaspoon dried basil
- ⅛ teaspoon grated nutmeg
- Sea salt, to taste
- Ground black pepper, to taste
- 2 pita bread

Directions:
1. Combine together the ground chicken, egg, stale bread slice, fresh garlic, Romano cheese, bell pepper, olive oil, oregano, basil, nutmeg, salt, and black pepper thoroughly in a mixing bowl. Stir well.
2. Lightly grease an air fryer basket.
3. Make 6 meatballs from the mixture and arrange the meatballs inside the air fryer basket.
4. Cook the meatballs in your air fryer at 390 degrees F/ 200 degrees C for 10 minutes. During cooking, shake the basket from time to time to cook evenly.
5. When cooked, add the keftedes inside the pita bread.
6. If desired, serve the meal with tomato and tzatziki sauce.

Fajita Stuffed Chicken Roll-ups

Servings: 4
Cooking Time: 25 Minutes
Ingredients:
- 2 (4-ounce) boneless, skinless chicken breasts
- Juice of ½ lime
- 2 tablespoons taco or fajita seasoning
- ½ red bell pepper, cut into strips
- ½ green bell pepper, cut into strips
- ¼ onion, sliced
- Cooking oil

Directions:
1. With your knife blade parallel to the cutting board, slice the chicken breasts in half horizontally to create 4 thin cutlets.
2. Drizzle the lime juice over the chicken cutlets, then season with the taco or fajita seasoning.
3. Place equal amounts of the red bell pepper strips, green bell pepper strips, and onion slices onto each of the chicken cutlets.
4. Roll up each cutlet and secure with toothpicks. The chicken will look like a cylinder.
5. Place 4 chicken roll-ups in the air fryer. Do not overcrowd the basket. Spray the chicken with cooking oil. Cook for 12 minutes.
6. Cool before serving.

Crunchy Chicken And Ranch Wraps

Servings: 4
Cooking Time: 25 Minutes
Ingredients:
- 2 (4-ounce) boneless, skinless breasts
- ½ (1-ounce) packet Hidden Valley Ranch seasoning mix
- Chicken seasoning or rub
- 1 cup all-purpose flour
- 1 egg
- ½ cup bread crumbs
- Cooking oil
- 4 medium (8-inch) flour tortillas
- 1½ cups shredded lettuce
- 3 tablespoons ranch dressing

Directions:
1. With your knife blade parallel to the cutting board, slice the chicken breasts in half horizontally to create 4 thin cutlets.
2. Season the chicken cutlets with the ranch seasoning and chicken seasoning to taste.
3. In a bowl large enough to dip a chicken cutlet, beat the egg. In another bowl, place the flour. Put the bread crumbs in a third bowl.
4. Spray the air fryer basket with cooking oil.
5. Dip each chicken cutlet in the flour, then the egg, and then the bread crumbs.
6. Place the chicken in the air fryer. Do not stack. Cook in batches. Spray the chicken with cooking oil. Cook for 7 minutes.
7. Open the air fryer and flip the chicken. Cook for an additional 3 to 4 minutes, until crisp.
8. Remove the cooked chicken from the air fryer and allow to cool for 2 to 3 minutes.
9. Repeat steps 6 through 8 for the remaining chicken.
10. Cut the chicken into strips. Divide the chicken strips, shredded lettuce, and ranch dressing evenly among the tortillas and serve.

Healthy Vegetable Patties

Servings: 6
Cooking Time: 10 Minutes
Ingredients:
- ¼ teaspoon black pepper
- ½ teaspoon paprika
- ¾ teaspoon salt
- 1 onion, chopped
- 1 teaspoon garlic powder
- 1 teaspoon onion powder
- 1-pound radish, peeled and grated
- 3 tablespoons coconut oil

Directions:
1. At 350 degrees F/ 175 degrees C, preheat your Air Fryer.
2. Place all the recipe ingredients in a suitable mixing bowl.
3. Form patties using your hands and place individual patties in the air fryer basket.
4. Spray with cooking spray before closing the air fryer.
5. Cook for 10 minutes at 350 degrees F/ 175 degrees C or until crispy.
6. When done, serve and enjoy.

Barbecued Chicken

Servings: 4
Cooking Time:18 To 20 Minutes
Ingredients:
- ⅓ cup no-salt-added tomato sauce
- 2 tablespoons low-sodium grainy mustard
- 2 tablespoons apple cider vinegar
- 1 tablespoon honey
- 2 garlic cloves, minced
- 1 jalapeño pepper, minced
- 3 tablespoons minced onion
- 4 (5-ounce) low-sodium boneless skinless chicken breasts (see Tip)

Directions:
1. In a small bowl, stir together the tomato sauce, mustard, cider vinegar, honey, garlic, jalapeño, and onion.
2. Brush the chicken breasts with some sauce and grill for 10 minutes.
3. Remove the air fryer basket and turn the chicken; brush with more sauce. Grill for 5 minutes more.
4. Remove the air fryer basket and turn the chicken again; brush with more sauce. Grill for 3 to 5 minutes more, or until the chicken reaches an internal temperature of 165°F on a meat thermometer. Discard any remaining sauce. Serve immediately.

Crispy Chicken Nuggets With Turnip

Servings: 3
Cooking Time: 32 Minutes
Ingredients:
- 1 egg
- ½ teaspoon cayenne pepper
- ⅓ cup panko crumbs
- ¼ teaspoon Romano cheese, grated
- 2 teaspoons canola oil
- 1 pound chicken breast, cut into slices
- 1 medium-sized turnip, trimmed and sliced
- ½ teaspoon garlic powder
- Sea salt, to taste
- Ground black pepper, to taste

Directions:
1. Whisk the egg together with the cayenne pepper until frothy in a bowl.
2. Mix the cheese together with the panko crumbs in another shallow until well combined.
3. Dredge the chicken slices firstly in the egg mixture, then in the panko mixture until coat well.
4. Then using 1 teaspoon of canola oil brush the slices.
5. To season, add salt and pepper.
6. Before cooking, heat your air fryer to 380 degrees F/ 195 degrees C.
7. Cook the chicken slices in the air fryer for 12 minutes. Shake the basket halfway through cooking.
8. When done, the internal temperature of their thickest part should read 165 degrees F/ 75 degrees C.
9. Remove from the air fryer and reserve. Keep warm.
10. With the remaining canola oil, drizzle over the turnip slices.
11. To season, add salt, pepper, and garlic powder.
12. Cook the slices in your air fryer at 370 degrees F/ 185 degrees C for about 20 minutes.
13. Serve the parsnip slices with chicken nuggets. Enjoy!

Classical Buffalo Wings

Servings: 4
Cooking Time: 22 Minutes
Ingredients:
- 1 ½ pounds chicken wings
- Coarse salt and ground black pepper, to season
- ½ teaspoon onion powder
- ½ teaspoon cayenne pepper
- 1 teaspoon granulated garlic
- 4 tablespoons butter, at room temperature
- 2 tablespoons hot pepper sauce
- 1 (1-inch) piece ginger, peeled and grated
- 2 tablespoons soy sauce
- 2 tablespoons molasses

Directions:
1. Using kitchen towels, dry the chicken wings and then set aside.
2. To season, add pepper, salt, cayenne pepper, granule garlic, and onion powder to toss the chicken wings.
3. Place the seasoned chicken wings evenly in the air fryer basket.
4. Cook in your air fryer at 380 degrees F/ 195 degrees C for 22 minutes until both sides are golden brown.
5. Meanwhile, mix together hot pepper sauce, soy sauce, molasses, butter, and ginger.
6. Drizzle the sauce mixture over the chicken wings.
7. Serve hot. Enjoy!

Cranberry Turkey Quesadillas

Servings: 4
Cooking Time: 4 To 8 Minutes
Ingredients:
- 6 low-sodium whole-wheat tortillas
- ⅓ cup shredded low-sodium low-fat Swiss cheese
- ¾ cup shredded cooked low-sodium turkey breast
- 2 tablespoons cranberry sauce
- 2 tablespoons dried cranberries
- ½ teaspoon dried basil
- Olive oil spray, for spraying the tortillas

Directions:
1. Put 3 tortillas on a work surface.
2. Evenly divide the Swiss cheese, turkey, cranberry sauce, and dried cranberries among the tortillas. Sprinkle with the basil and top with the remaining tortillas.
3. Spray the outsides of the tortillas with olive oil spray.
4. One at a time, grill the quesadillas in the air fryer for 4 to 8 minutes, or until crisp and the cheese is melted. Cut into quarters and serve.

Fried Buffalo Chicken Taquitos

Servings: 6
Cooking Time: 5 To 10 Minutes
Ingredients:
- 8 ounces (227 g) fat-free cream cheese, softened
- ⅛ cup Buffalo sauce
- 2 cups shredded cooked chicken
- 12 (7-inch) low-carb flour tortillas
- Olive oil spray

Directions:
1. Preheat the air fryer to 360°F (182°C). Spray the air fryer basket lightly with olive oil spray.
2. In a large bowl, mix together the cream cheese and Buffalo sauce until well combined. Add the chicken and stir until combined.
3. Place the tortillas on a clean workspace. Spoon 2 to 3 tablespoons of the chicken mixture in a thin line down the center of each tortilla. Roll up the tortillas.
4. Place the tortillas in the air fryer basket, seam-side down. Spray each tortilla lightly with olive oil spray. You may need to cook the taquitos in batches.
5. Air fry until golden brown, 5 to 10 minutes. Serve hot.

Dill Chicken Strips

Servings: 4
Cooking Time: 10 Minutes
Ingredients:
- 2 whole boneless, skinless chicken breasts, halved lengthwise
- 1 cup Italian dressing
- 3 cups finely crushed potato chips
- 1 tablespoon dried dill weed
- 1 tablespoon garlic powder
- 1 large egg, beaten
- Cooking spray

Directions:
1. In a large resealable bag, combine the chicken and Italian dressing. Seal the bag and refrigerate to marinate at least 1 hour.
2. In a shallow dish, stir together the potato chips, dill, and garlic powder. Place the beaten egg in a second shallow dish.
3. Remove the chicken from the marinade. Roll the chicken pieces in the egg and the potato chip mixture, coating thoroughly.
4. Preheat the air fryer to 325°F (163°C). Line the air fryer basket with parchment paper.
5. Place the coated chicken on the parchment and spritz with cooking spray.
6. Bake for 5 minutes. Flip the chicken, spritz it with cooking spray, and bake for 5 minutes more until the outsides are crispy and the insides are no longer pink. Serve immediately.

Lemon Chicken In Oyster Sauce

Servings: 4-5
Cooking Time: 20 Minutes
Ingredients:
- 1 tablespoon oyster sauce
- 1 teaspoon lemon juice
- 2 ½ tablespoons maple syrup
- 1 tablespoon tamari soy sauce
- 1 teaspoon fresh ginger, minced
- 1 teaspoon garlic puree
- Seasoned salt and ground pepper as needed
- 2 chicken breasts, boneless and skinless

Directions:
1. Combine together tamari sauce, oyster sauce, ginger, garlic puree, syrup, and lemon juice in a deep dish.
2. To season, toss the chicken with salt and pepper.
3. To marinate, combine the chicken and the tamari mixture in a zip-lock bag. Seal the bag and cook in the refrigerator for 3 to 4 hours.
4. On a flat kitchen surface, plug your air fryer and turn it on.
5. Before cooking, heat your air fryer to 365 degrees F/ 185 degrees C for 4 to 5 minutes.
6. Gently grease an air fryer basket with cooking oil or spray.
7. Place the marinated chicken in the air fryer basket.
8. Insert the basket inside the air fryer and cook for 7 minutes.
9. Then flip the chicken and cook the other side for 7 minutes.
10. Add the marinade to a saucepan and simmer to thicken to half.
11. When cooked, serve the chicken with warm marinade sauce.

Herbs Chicken Drumsticks With Tamari Sauce

Servings: 6
Cooking Time: 35 Minutes
Ingredients:
- 6 chicken drumsticks
- Sauce:
- 6 oz. hot sauce
- 3 tablespoons olive oil
- 3 tablespoons tamari sauce
- 1 teaspoon dried thyme
- ½ teaspoon dried oregano

Directions:
1. Spritz a nonstick cooking spray over the sides and bottom of the cooking basket.
2. Cook the chicken drumsticks at 380 degrees F/ 195 degrees C for 35 minutes, flipping them over halfway through.
3. Meanwhile, heat the hot sauce, olive oil, tamari sauce, thyme, and oregano in a pan over medium-low heat; reserve.
4. Drizzle the sauce over the prepared chicken drumsticks; toss to coat well and serve.

Seasoned Chicken Breast

Servings: 4
Cooking Time: 20 Minutes
Ingredients:
- 1-pound chicken breast, skinless, boneless, and cut into chunks
- 2 cups broccoli florets
- 2 teaspoons hot sauce
- 2 teaspoons vinegar
- 1 teaspoon sesame oil
- 1 tablespoon soy sauce
- 1 tablespoon ginger, minced
- ½ teaspoon garlic powder
- 1 tablespoon olive oil
- ½ onion, sliced
- Black pepper
- Salt

Directions:
1. Add all the recipe ingredients into the suitable mixing bowl and toss well.
2. Grease its air fryer basket with cooking spray.
3. Transfer chicken and broccoli mixture into the air fryer basket.
4. Cook at almost 380 degrees F/ 195 degrees C for almost 15-20 minutes. Shake halfway through.
5. Serve and enjoy.

Italian Chicken And Veggies

Servings: 4
Cooking Time: 30 Minutes
Ingredients:
- ¾ cup balsamic vinaigrette dressing, divided
- 1 pound boneless, skinless chicken tenderloins
- Olive oil
- 1 pound fresh green beans, trimmed
- 1 pint grape tomatoes

Directions:
1. Place ½ cup of the balsamic vinaigrette dressing and the chicken in a large zip-top plastic bag, seal, and refrigerate for at least 1 hour or up to overnight.
2. In a large bowl, mix together the green beans, tomatoes, and the remaining ¼ cup of balsamic vinaigrette dressing until well coated.
3. Spray the fryer basket lightly with oil. Place the vegetables in the fryer basket. Reserve any remaining vinaigrette.
4. Air fry for 8 minutes. Shake the basket and continue to cook until the beans are crisp but tender, and the tomatoes are soft and slightly charred, an additional 5 to 7 minutes.
5. Wipe the fryer basket with a paper towel and spray lightly with olive oil.
6. Place the chicken in the fryer basket in a single layer. You may need to cook them in batches.
7. Air fry for 7 minutes. Flip the chicken over, baste with some of the remaining vinaigrette, and cook until the chicken reaches an internal temperature of 165°F, an additional 5 to 8 minutes.
8. Serve the chicken and veggies together.

Rotisserie Whole Chicken

Servings: 6 Servings
Cooking Time: 1 Hour 5 Minutes
Ingredients:
- 1 whole chicken without giblets (about 5 pounds)
- 1 tablespoon of salt
- 1 teaspoon of garlic powder
- 1 teaspoon of black pepper
- 1 teaspoon of smoked paprika
- ½ teaspoon of dried oregano
- ½ teaspoon of dried basil
- ½ teaspoon of dried thyme
- 2 tablespoons of olive oil

Directions:
1. Preheat your air fryer to 360°F.
2. Mix all seasonings with oil in a mixing bowl and spread it over the chicken.
3. Spray the air fryer basket with cooking spray. Put the chicken breast-side down in the air fryer basket and cook for 50 minutes. Flip it and cook at 360°F for 10 minutes more. If chicken is not 165°F internally, cook for additional 5–10 minutes.
4. Serve warm and enjoy your Rotisserie Whole Chicken!

Bruschetta-stuffed Chicken

Servings: 4
Cooking Time: 20 Minutes
Ingredients:
- For the bruschetta stuffing
- 2 tablespoons extra-virgin olive oil
- 3 tablespoons balsamic vinegar
- 3 garlic cloves, minced
- 1 tomato, diced
- 1 teaspoon Italian seasoning
- 2 tablespoons chopped fresh basil
- For the chicken
- 4 (4-ounce) boneless, skinless chicken breasts
- 1 teaspoon Italian seasoning
- Chicken seasoning or rub
- Cooking oil

Directions:
1. Cut 4 or 5 slits into each chicken breast, without cutting all the way through.
2. Season the chicken with the Italian seasoning and chicken seasoning to taste.
3. Spray the air fryer basket with cooking oil.
4. Place the chicken (with the slits facing up) in the air fryer. Do not stack. Cook in batches. Spray the chicken with cooking oil. Cook for 7 minutes.
5. Open the air fryer and stuff the bruschetta mixture into the slits of the chicken. Cook for an additional 3 minutes.
6. Remove the cooked chicken from the air fryer, then repeat steps 4 and 5 for the remaining chicken breasts.
7. Cool before serving.

Herbed Chicken And Broccoli

Servings: 6
Cooking Time: 15 Minutes
Ingredients:
- 3 tablespoons dried parsley, crushed
- 1 tablespoon onion powder
- 1 tablespoon garlic powder
- ½ teaspoon red chili powder
- ½ teaspoon paprika
- 2 pounds boneless, skinless chicken breasts, sliced
- 3 cups instant white rice
- ¾ cup cream soup
- 3 cups small broccoli florets
- ⅓ cup butter
- 3 cups water

Directions:
1. In a large mixing dish, add spices and the parsley together.
2. Dredge the chicken slices in the spice mixture until coat well.
3. Line 6 large foil pieces on a flat table.
4. Arrange ½ cup of rice over each foil piece. Then add the, 2 tablespoons of cream soup, ½ cup of broccoli, ⅙ of chicken, ½ cup of water, and 1 tablespoon of butter.
5. Then fold tightly the foil to ensure the rice mixture is sealed.
6. Arrange onto the air fryer basket.
7. Air fry the foil packets in your air fryer at 390 degrees F/ 200 degrees C for about 15 minutes.
8. When the cooking time runs out, remove from the air fryer and serve hot on plates.

Apricot-glazed Turkey Tenderloin

Servings: 4
Cooking Time: 30 Minutes
Ingredients:
- Olive oil
- ¼ cup sugar-free apricot preserves
- ½ tablespoon spicy brown mustard
- 1½ pound turkey breast tenderloin
- Salt
- Freshly ground black pepper

Directions:
1. Spray a fryer basket lightly with olive oil.
2. In a small bowl, combine the apricot preserves and mustard to make a paste.
3. Season the turkey with salt and pepper. Spread the apricot paste all over the turkey.
4. Place the turkey in the fryer basket and lightly spray with olive oil.
5. Air fry for 15 minutes. Flip the turkey over and lightly spray with olive oil. Air fry until the internal temperature reaches at least 170°F, an additional 10 to 15 minutes.
6. Let the turkey rest for 10 minutes before slicing and serving.

Crispy Chicken Wings

Servings: 4 Servings
Cooking Time: 40 Minutes
Ingredients:
- 2 pounds of chicken wings
- ½ cup of hot sauce
- 4 tablespoons of unsalted butter
- Pinch of salt and black pepper, to taste

Directions:
1. Spray the air fryer basket with cooking spray. Preheat it to 360°F.
2. Dry the chicken wings with a paper towel. Sprinkle them with salt and black pepper. Place wings in the basket. Avoid touching each other. Cook at 360°F for 12 minutes, flip them with tongs, and continue cooking for 12 minutes more. Flip again, increase the temperature to 390°F, and cook for about 6 minutes until crispy.
3. Meanwhile, warm butter in the microwave until fully melted. Mix in the hot sauce.
4. Coat the cooked wings with the butter-sauce mixture.
5. Serve warm* and enjoy your Crispy Chicken Wings!

Blackened Chicken Breasts

Servings: 4
Cooking Time: 20 Minutes
Ingredients:
- 1 large egg, beaten
- ¾ cup Blackened seasoning
- 2 whole boneless, skinless chicken breasts (about 1 pound / 454 g each), halved
- Cooking spray

Directions:
1. Preheat the air fryer to 360°F (182°C). Line the air fryer basket with parchment paper.
2. Place the beaten egg in one shallow bowl and the Blackened seasoning in another shallow bowl.
3. One at a time, dip the chicken pieces in the beaten egg and the Blackened seasoning, coating thoroughly.
4. Place the chicken pieces on the parchment and spritz with cooking spray.
5. Air fry for 10 minutes. Flip the chicken, spritz it with cooking spray, and air fry for 10 minutes more until the internal temperature reaches 165°F (74°C) and the chicken is no longer pink inside. Let sit for 5 minutes before serving.

Spicy Asian Chicken Thighs With Soy Sauce

Servings: 4
Cooking Time: 20 Minutes
Ingredients:
- 4 chicken thighs, skin-on, and bone-in
- 2 teaspoons ginger, grated
- 1 lime juice
- 2 tablespoons chili garlic sauce
- ¼ cup olive oil
- ⅓ cup soy sauce

Directions:
1. In a suitable bowl, whisk together chili garlic sauce, ginger, lime juice, soy sauce oil.
2. Add chicken to the same bowl and coat well with the prepared marinade, cover and place in the refrigerator for almost 30 minutes.
3. Set marinated chicken in your air fryer basket and air fryer at 400 degrees F/ 205 degrees C for 15-20 minutes.
4. Serve and enjoy.

Chicken And Onion Sausages

Servings: 4
Cooking Time: 10 Minutes
Ingredients:
- 1 garlic clove, diced
- 1 spring onion, chopped
- 1 cup ground chicken
- ½ teaspoon salt
- ½ teaspoon ground black pepper
- 4 sausage links
- 1 teaspoon olive oil

Directions:
1. Mix together the ground chicken, ground black pepper, onion, and the diced garlic clove in a mixing dish to make the filling.
2. Fill the sausage links with the chicken mixture.
3. Then cut the sausages into halves and make sure the endings of the sausage halves are secured.
4. Before cooking, heat your air fryer to 365 degrees F/ 185 degrees C.
5. Brush olive oil over the sausages. Arrange the chicken and onion sausage in the air fryer basket and cook in the preheated air fryer for 10 minutes.
6. Then flip the sausage to ensure even cook. Cook again for 5 minutes or more. Or increase the temperature to 390 degrees F/ 200 degrees C and cook for 8 minutes for a faster result.

Alfredo Chicken With Mushrooms

Servings: 3
Cooking Time: 15 Minutes
Ingredients:
- 1 pound chicken breasts, boneless
- 1 medium onion, quartered
- 1 teaspoon butter, melted
- ½ pound mushrooms, cleaned
- 12 ounces Alfredo sauce
- Salt and black pepper, to taste

Directions:
1. Before cooking, heat your air fryer to 380 degrees F/ 195 degrees C.
2. In the air fryer basket, add the onion and chicken and drizzle over with melted butter.
3. Cook for 6 minutes. When the cooking time is up, add mushrooms in the air fryer basket and cook again for 5 to 6 minutes or more.
4. Cut the chicken into strips. Add the chopped mushrooms and onions and stir in the Alfredo sauce. Add pepper and salt as you desired to taste.
5. Serve the chicken with the hot cooked fettuccine. Enjoy!

Sesame Chicken Tenders

Servings: 4
Cooking Time: 15 Minutes
Ingredients:
- Olive oil
- ¼ cup soy sauce
- 2 tablespoons white vinegar
- 1 tablespoon honey
- 1 tablespoon toasted sesame oil
- 1 tablespoon lime juice
- 1 teaspoon ground ginger
- 1 pound boneless skinless, chicken tenderloins
- 2 teaspoon toasted sesame seeds

Directions:
1. Spray a fryer basket lightly with olive oil.
2. In a large zip-top plastic bag, combine the soy sauce, white vinegar, honey, sesame oil, lime juice, and ginger to make a marinade.
3. Add the chicken tenderloins to the bag, seal, and marinate the chicken in the refrigerator for at least 2 hours or overnight.
4. If using wooden skewers, soak them in water for at least 30 minutes before using.
5. Thread 1 chicken tenderloin onto each skewer. Sprinkle with sesame seeds. Reserve the marinade.
6. Place the skewers in the fryer basket in a single layer. You may need to cook the chicken in batches.
7. Air fry for 6 minutes. Flip the chicken over, baste with more marinade, and cook until crispy, an additional 5 to 8 minutes.

Spicy And Crispy Duck

Servings: 3
Cooking Time: 20 Minutes
Ingredients:
- 2 tablespoons peanuts, chopped
- 1 tablespoon honey
- 1 tablespoon olive oil
- 1 tablespoon hoisin sauce
- 1 pound duck breast
- 1 small-sized white onion, sliced
- 1 teaspoon garlic, chopped
- 1 celery stick, diced
- 1 thumb ginger, sliced
- 4 baby potatoes, diced

Directions:
1. Using cooking oil, lightly grease the air fryer basket.
2. In a mixing bowl, combine honey, hoisin sauce, peanuts, and olive oil.
3. Rub the duck breast with mixture and transfer to the air fryer basket.
4. Spread garlic, celery, potatoes, ginger and onion over the duck breast.
5. Cook at 400 degrees F/ 205 degrees C for 20 minutes.
6. Serve the duck breast with Mandarin pancakes.

Chicken And Carrot

Servings: 4
Cooking Time: 30-35 Minutes
Ingredients:
- 2 chicken breasts, make bite-sized chunks
- 1 cup scallions, chopped
- 1 parsnip, chopped
- ⅓ cup cornstarch
- ⅓ cup flour
- 1 carrot, thinly sliced
- For the Sauce:
- ¼ cup dry white wine
- ¼ cup soy sauce
- ¼ cup honey
- ⅓ cup chicken broth

Directions:
1. On a flat kitchen surface, plug your air fryer and turn it on.
2. Before cooking, heat your air fryer to 365 degrees F/ 185 degrees C for about 4 to 5 minutes. Gently coat the air fryer basket with cooking oil or spray.
3. Mix thoroughly the cornstarch, flour, and chicken chunks.
4. Place the chicken to the air fryer basket.
5. Cook in your air fryer for 20 minutes.
6. When cooked, remove from the air fryer and add the veggies.
7. Cook for 7 minutes.
8. To make the sauce, whisk the sauce ingredients in a saucepan over moderate heat.
9. Serve the chicken with the sauce.

Chicken Fillets With Lemon Pepper & Cheddar Cheese

Servings: 2
Cooking Time: 14 Minutes
Ingredients:
- 1 lemon pepper
- ¼ cup Cheddar cheese, shredded
- 8 oz. chicken fillets
- ½ teaspoon dried cilantro
- 1 teaspoon coconut oil, melted
- ¼ teaspoon smoked paprika

Directions:
1. Cut the lemon pepper into halves and remove the seeds.
2. Then cut the chicken fillet into 2 fillets.
3. Make the horizontal cuts in every chicken fillet.
4. Then sprinkle the chicken fillets with smoked paprika and dried cilantro. After this, fill them with lemon pepper halves and Cheddar cheese.
5. At 385 degrees F/ 195 degrees C, preheat your air fryer.
6. Put the chicken fillets in the preheated Air Fryer and sprinkle with melted coconut oil. Cook the chicken for 14 minutes.
7. Carefully transfer the chicken fillets in the serving plates.
8. Serve.

Mexican Sheet Pan Dinner

Servings: 4
Cooking Time: 15 Minutes
Ingredients:
- 1 pound boneless, skinless chicken tenderloins, cut into strips
- 3 bell peppers, any color, cut into chunks
- 1 onion, cut into chunks
- 1 tablespoon olive oil, plus more for spraying
- 1 tablespoon fajita seasoning mix

Directions:
1. In a large bowl, mix together the chicken, bell peppers, onion, 1 tablespoon of olive oil, and fajita seasoning mix until completely coated.
2. Spray a fryer basket lightly with olive oil.
3. Place the chicken and vegetables in the fryer basket and lightly spray with olive oil.
4. Air fry for 7 minutes. Shake the basket and cook until the chicken is cooked through and the veggies are starting to char, an additional 5 to 8 minutes.

Grilled Chicken With Salsa Verde

Servings: 2
Cooking Time: 40 Minutes
Ingredients:
- ½ red onion, chopped
- ½ teaspoon chili powder
- 1 jalapeno thinly sliced
- 1 jar salsa Verde, divided
- 1-pound boneless skinless chicken breasts
- 2 cloves of garlic, minced
- 2 tablespoons chopped cilantro
- 2 tablespoons extra virgin olive oil
- 4 slices Monterey Jack cheese
- Juice from ½ lime
- Lime wedges for serving

Directions:
1. In a Ziploc bag, add ½ of the salsa Verde, olive oil, lime juice, garlic, chili powder and chicken.
2. Let this chicken marinate in the fridge for at least 2 hours.
3. At 390 degrees F/ 200 degrees C, preheat your Air fryer.
4. Set a suitable grill pan accessory in the air fryer basket.
5. Cook the prepared chicken in your air fryer for 40 minutes almost.
6. Flip the chicken every 10 minutes to cook evenly.
7. Serve the chicken with the cheese, jalapeno, red onion, cilantro, and lime wedges.

Tex-mex Turkey Burgers

Servings: 4
Cooking Time: 14 To 16 Minutes
Ingredients:
- ⅓ cup finely crushed corn tortilla chips
- 1 egg, beaten
- ¼ cup salsa
- ⅓ cup shredded pepper Jack cheese
- Pinch salt
- Freshly ground black pepper, to taste
- 1 pound (454 g) ground turkey
- 1 tablespoon olive oil
- 1 teaspoon paprika

Directions:
1. Preheat the air fryer to 330°F (166°C).
2. In a medium bowl, combine the tortilla chips, egg, salsa, cheese, salt, and pepper, and mix well.
3. Add the turkey and mix gently but thoroughly with clean hands.
4. Form the meat mixture into patties about ½ inch thick. Make an indentation in the center of each patty with your thumb so the burgers don't puff up while cooking.
5. Brush the patties on both sides with the olive oil and sprinkle with paprika.
6. Put in the air fryer basket and air fry for 14 to 16 minutes or until the meat registers at least 165°F (74°C).
7. Let sit for 5 minutes before serving.

Beef, Pork & Lamb Recipes

Lamb Burger

Servings: 4
Cooking Time: 16 Minutes
Ingredients:
- 2 teaspoons olive oil
- ⅓ onion, finely chopped
- 1 clove garlic, minced
- 1 pound (454 g) ground lamb
- 2 tablespoons fresh parsley, finely chopped
- 1½ teaspoons fresh oregano, finely chopped
- ½ cup black olives, finely chopped
- ⅓ cup crumbled feta cheese
- ½ teaspoon salt
- freshly ground black pepper
- 4 thick pita breads
- toppings and condiments

Directions:
1. Preheat a medium skillet over medium-high heat on the stovetop. Add the olive oil and cook the onion until tender, but not browned about 4 to 5 minutes. Add the garlic and cook for another minute. Transfer the onion and garlic to a mixing bowl and add the ground lamb, parsley, oregano, olives, feta cheese, salt and pepper. Gently mix the ingredients together.
2. Divide the mixture into 3 or 4 equal portions and then form the hamburgers, being careful not to over-handle the meat. One good way to do this is to throw the meat back and forth between the hands like a baseball, packing the meat each time you catch it. Flatten the balls into patties, making an indentation in the center of each patty. Flatten the sides of the patties as well to make it easier to fit them into the air fryer basket.
3. Preheat the air fryer to 370°F (188°C).
4. If you don't have room for all four burgers, air fry two or three burgers at a time for 8 minutes. Flip the burgers over and air fry for another 8 minutes. If you cooked the burgers in batches, return the first batch of burgers to the air fryer for the last two minutes of cooking to re-heat. This should give you a medium-well burger. If you'd prefer a medium-rare burger, shorten the cooking time to about 13 minutes. Remove the burgers to a resting plate and let the burgers rest for a few minutes before dressing and serving.
5. While the burgers are resting, bake the pita breads in the air fryer for 2 minutes. Tuck the burgers into the toasted pita breads, or wrap the pitas around the burgers and serve with a tzatziki sauce or some mayonnaise.

Meatballs In Spicy Tomato Sauce

Servings: 4
Cooking Time: 11 To 15 Minutes
Ingredients:
- 3 green onions, minced
- 1 garlic clove, minced
- 1 egg yolk
- ¼ cup saltine cracker crumbs
- Pinch salt
- Freshly ground black pepper
- 1 pound 95 percent lean ground beef
- Olive oil for misting
- 1¼ cups pasta sauce (from a 16-ounce jar)
- 2 tablespoons Dijon mustard

Directions:
1. In a large bowl, combine the green onions, garlic, egg yolk, cracker crumbs, salt, and pepper, and mix well.
2. Add the ground beef and mix gently but thoroughly with your hands until combined. Form into 1½-inch meatballs.
3. Mist the meatballs with olive oil and put into the basket of the air fryer.
4. Bake for 8 to 11 minutes or until the meatballs are 165°F.
5. Remove the meatballs from the basket and place in a 6-inch metal bowl. Top with the pasta sauce and Dijon mustard and mix gently.
6. Bake for 3 to 4 minutes or until the sauce is hot.

Creole Pork Chops

Servings: 4
Cooking Time: 12 Minutes
Ingredients:
- 1 ½ lbs. pork chops, boneless
- 1 teaspoon garlic powder
- 5-tablespoon parmesan cheese, grated
- ⅓ cup almond flour
- 1 ½-teaspoon paprika
- 1 teaspoon Creole seasoning

Directions:
1. Heat the air fryer to 360 degrees F/ 180 degrees C in advance.
2. In a zip-lock bag, in addition to the pork chops, mix the other ingredients well.
3. Add pork chops into the bag and coat it with the mixture well by shaking the bag.
4. Coat the basket of your air fryer with cooking spray.
5. Place pork chops into the air fryer basket and cook for 12 minutes at 360 degrees F/ 180 degrees C.
6. Serve and enjoy.

Pork Tenderloin With Bell Pepper

Servings: 2
Cooking Time: 18 Minutes
Ingredients:
- 1 red onion, make thin slices
- 1 yellow or red bell pepper, make thin strips
- 2 teaspoons herbs
- 1 tablespoon olive oil
- ½ tablespoon mustard
- Black pepper, ground as required
- 11-ounce pork tenderloin

Directions:
1. Make the tenderloin into four pieces, spread the oil, mustard and sprinkle some pepper and salt on them.
2. Thoroughly mix the herbs, pepper strips, oil, onion, salt and pepper in a medium-size bowl.
3. Coat the cooking basket of your air fryer with cooking oil or spray.
4. Add the mixture on the basket, put the tenderloin pieces on and then arrange the basket to the air fryer.
5. Cook the tenderloin pieces at 390 degrees F/ 200 degrees C for 16-18 minutes.
6. When done, serve warm!

Spiced Pork Chops

Servings: 2
Cooking Time: 20 Minutes
Ingredients:
- 1 tablespoon olive oil
- ½ lb. pork chops
- ½ teaspoon dried oregano
- ¼ teaspoon red pepper flakes
- 1 teaspoon dried thyme
- ½ teaspoon salt
- ½ teaspoon pepper
- 6 large mushrooms, cleaned and sliced
- 1 large yellow onion, chopped
- 1 ½ tablespoons soy sauce
- 2 tablespoons fresh parsley, finely chopped

Directions:
1. Mix the pork chops with the onion, mushrooms, pepper, red pepper flakes, thyme, oregano, olive oil, soy sauce, and olive oil in a large bowl.
2. When coated, cook the pork chops and clean mushrooms in your air fryer at 390 degrees F/ 200 degrees C for 20 minutes.
3. Sprinkle with the fresh parsley, serve and enjoy!

Burgundy Beef Dish With Egg Noodles

Servings: 5
Cooking Time: 25 Minutes
Ingredients:
- 1 package egg noodles, cooked
- 1 oz. dry onion soup mix
- 1 can (14.5 oz.) cream mushroom soup
- 2 cups mushrooms, sliced
- 1 whole onion, chopped
- ½ cup beef broth
- 3 garlic cloves, minced

Directions:
1. At 360 degrees F/ 180 degrees C, preheat your air fryer.
2. Drizzle onion soup mix all over the meat.
3. In a suitable mixing bowl, mix the sauce, garlic cloves, beef broth, chopped onion, sliced mushrooms and mushroom soup.
4. Top the meat with the prepared sauce mixture.
5. Place the prepared meat in the air fryer's cooking basket and cook for 25 minutes.
6. Serve with cooked egg noodles.

Beef Taco Chimichangas

Servings: 4
Cooking Time: 20 Minutes
Ingredients:
- Cooking oil
- ½ cup chopped onion
- 2 garlic cloves, minced
- 1 pound 93% lean ground beef
- 2 tablespoons taco seasoning
- Salt
- Pepper
- 1 (15-ounce) can diced tomatoes with chiles
- 4 medium (8-inch) flour tortillas
- 1 cup shredded Cheddar cheese (a blend of ½ cup shredded Cheddar and ½ cup shredded Monterey Jack works great, too)

Directions:
1. Spray a skillet with cooking oil and place over medium-high heat. Add the chopped onion and garlic. Cook for 2 to 3 minutes, until fragrant.
2. Add the ground beef, taco seasoning, and salt and pepper to taste. Use a large spoon or spatula to break up the beef. Cook for 2 to 4 minutes, until browned.
3. Add the diced tomatoes with chiles. Stir to combine.
4. Mound ½ cup of the ground beef mixture on each of the tortillas.
5. To form the chimichangas, fold the sides of the tortilla in toward the middle and then roll up from the bottom. You can secure the chimichanga with a toothpick. Or you can moisten the upper edge of the tortilla with a small amount of water before sealing. I prefer to use a cooking brush, but you can dab with your fingers.
6. Spray the chimichangas with cooking oil.
7. Place the chimichangas in the air fryer. Do not stack. Cook in batches. Cook for 8 minutes.
8. Remove the cooked chimichangas from the air fryer and top them with the shredded cheese. The heat from the chimichangas will melt the cheese.
9. Repeat steps 7 and 8 for the remaining chimichangas, and serve.

Spiced Lamb Kebabs

Servings: 3
Cooking Time: 60 Minutes
Ingredients:
- 1 ½ pounds lamb shoulder, bones removed and cut into pieces
- 2 tablespoons cumin seeds, toasted
- 2 teaspoons caraway seeds, toasted
- 1 tablespoon Sichuan peppercorns
- 1 teaspoon sugar
- 2 teaspoons crushed red pepper flakes
- Salt and pepper

Directions:
1. In a suitable bowl, add all of the ingredients, stir well and refrigerate for at least 2 hours to marinate the lamb shoulder pieces completely.
2. Cook the marinated pieces at 390 degrees F/ 200 degrees C for 15 minutes.
3. After 8 minutes, flip the pieces for even grilling and then cook for 7 minutes more.
4. Working in batches is suggested.
5. When done, serve warm and enjoy.

Best Damn Pork Chops

Servings: 2 Servings
Cooking Time: 20 Minutes
Ingredients:
- 2 bone-in 2-inch-thick pork chops
- 2 tablespoons of brown sugar
- 1 teaspoon of ground mustard
- ¼ teaspoon of garlic powder
- ½ teaspoon of onion powder
- 1 tablespoon of paprika
- 1 ½ teaspoons of black pepper
- 1 ½ teaspoons of salt
- 1–2 tablespoons olive oil

Directions:
1. Preheat your air fryer to 400°F.
2. Rinse the pork chops and dry with a paper towel.
3. Add sugar, mustard, garlic and onion powder, paprika, salt, and black pepper in a bowl. Mix it well.
4. Grease the pork chops with olive oil and coat them with seasonings. Use almost all the rub mix.
5. Put the prepared pork chops in the preheated air fryer basket and cook at 400°F for 12 minutes, flip them, and cook for extra 6 minutes.
6. Serve warm and enjoy your Best Damn Pork Chops!

Lamb Meatballs

Servings: 4
Cooking Time: 8 Minutes
Ingredients:
- Meatballs:
- ½ small onion, finely diced
- 1 clove garlic, minced
- 1 pound (454 g) ground lamb
- 2 tablespoons fresh parsley, finely chopped (plus more for garnish)
- 2 teaspoons fresh oregano, finely chopped
- 2 tablespoons milk
- 1 egg yolk
- Salt and freshly ground black pepper, to taste
- ½ cup crumbled feta cheese, for garnish
- Tomato Sauce:
- 2 tablespoons butter
- 1 clove garlic, smashed
- Pinch crushed red pepper flakes
- ¼ teaspoon ground cinnamon
- 1 (28-ounce / 794-g) can crushed tomatoes
- Salt, to taste
- Olive oil, for greasing

Directions:
1. Combine all ingredients for the meatballs in a large bowl and mix just until everything is combined. Shape the mixture into 1½-inch balls or shape the meat between two spoons to make quenelles.
2. Preheat the air fryer to 400°F (204°C).
3. While the air fryer is preheating, start the quick tomato sauce. Put the butter, garlic and red pepper flakes in a sauté pan and heat over medium heat on the stovetop. Let the garlic sizzle a little, but before the butter browns, add the cinnamon and tomatoes. Bring to a simmer and simmer for 15 minutes. Season with salt.
4. Grease the bottom of the air fryer basket with olive oil and transfer the meatballs to the air fryer basket in one layer, air frying in batches if necessary.
5. Air fry for 8 minutes, giving the basket a shake once during the cooking process to turn the meatballs over.
6. To serve, spoon a pool of the tomato sauce onto plates and add the meatballs. Sprinkle the feta cheese on top and garnish with more fresh parsley. Serve immediately.

Tomato Pork Burgers

Servings: 4
Cooking Time: 7 Minutes
Ingredients:
- ½ cup Greek yogurt
- 2 tablespoons mustard, divided
- 1 tablespoon lemon juice
- ¼ cup sliced red cabbage
- ¼ cup grated carrots
- 1-pound lean ground pork
- ½ teaspoon paprika
- 1 cup mixed baby lettuce greens
- 2 small tomatoes, sliced
- 8 small whole-wheat sandwich buns, cut in ½

Directions:
1. In a suitable bowl, combine the yogurt, 1 tablespoon mustard, lemon juice, cabbage, and carrots; mix and refrigerate.
2. In a suitable bowl, combine the pork, remaining 1 tablespoon mustard, and paprika. Form into 8 small patties.
3. Set the sliders into the air fryer basket and cook for 7 minutes.
4. Make the burgers by placing adding the lettuce greens on a bun.
5. Top it with a tomato slice, the burgers, and the cabbage mixture.
6. Add the bun top and serve immediately.

Mozzarella Beef Brisket

Servings: 6
Cooking Time: 25 Minutes
Ingredients:
- 12 ounces (340 g) beef brisket
- 2 teaspoons Italian herbs
- 2 teaspoons butter
- 1 onion, sliced
- 7 ounces (198 g) Mozzarella cheese, sliced

Directions:
1. Preheat the air fryer to 365°F (185°C).
2. Cut up the brisket into four equal slices and season with the Italian herbs.
3. Allow the butter to melt in the air fryer. Put the slices of beef inside along with the onion. Air fry for 25 minutes. Flip the brisket halfway through. Put a piece of Mozzarella on top of each piece of brisket in the last 5 minutes.
4. Serve immediately.

Steak Kabobs With Vegetables

Servings: 4
Cooking Time: 10 Minutes
Ingredients:
- 2 tablespoons light soy sauce
- 4 cups lean beef chuck ribs, cut into one-inch pieces
- ⅓ cup low-fat: sour cream:
- ½ onion
- 8 6-inch skewers:
- 1 bell peppers

Directions:
1. Mix well the soy sauce and sour cream in a suitable bowl, then add the lean beef chunks and coat well.
2. Marinate the chunks for 30 minutes.
3. Soak skewers for 10 minutes in boil water.
4. Cut onion and bell pepper in 1-inch pieces.
5. Add bell peppers, onions and beef chunks on skewers. You can also choose to sprinkle with black pepper.
6. Cook them in air fryer at 400 degrees F/ 205 degrees C for 10 minutes, flipping halfway through.
7. When done, serve with yogurt dipping sauce.

Glazed Beef With Fruits

Servings: 8
Cooking Time: 11 Minutes
Ingredients:
- 12 ounces sirloin tip steak, thinly sliced
- 1 tablespoon lime juice
- 1 cup canned mandarin orange segments, drained
- 1 cup canned pineapple chunks, drained
- 1 teaspoon soy sauce
- 1 tablespoon cornstarch
- 1 teaspoon olive oil
- 2 scallions, white and green parts, sliced
- Brown rice, cooked

Directions:
1. In a suitable bowl, mix the steak with the lime juice. Set aside.
2. In a suitable bowl, mix 3 tablespoons of reserved pineapple juice, 3 tablespoons of reserved mandarin orange juice, cornstarch and the soy sauce.
3. Drain the marinated beef and transfer it to a medium metal bowl, keep the juice aside.
4. Stir the reserved juice into the mandarin-pineapple juice mixture.
5. Drizzle the olive oil and scallions on the steak.
6. Set the metal bowl in the preheated Air Fryer and cook for 3 to 4 minutes.
7. Add the mandarin oranges, juicemixture and pineapple.
8. Cook for 3 to 7 minutes more.
9. Stir and serve.

Cube Steak

Servings: 4
Cooking Time: 20 Minutes
Ingredients:
- 1 ½ lbs. cube steak
- Salt, to taste
- ¼-teaspoon ground black pepper, or more to taste
- 4 ounces' butter
- 2 garlic cloves, finely chopped
- 2 scallions, finely chopped
- 2-tablespoon fresh parsley, finely chopped
- 1 tablespoon fresh horseradish, grated
- 1 teaspoon cayenne pepper

Directions:
1. Use the kitchen to pat the cube steak dry, then season it with salt and black pepper.
2. Coat the cooking basket of your air fryer with cooking oil or spray.
3. Place the cube steak on the basket and then arrange the basket to the air fryer.
4. Cook the cube steak at 400 degrees F/ 205 degrees C for 14 minutes.
5. While cooking the cube steak, melt the butter in a skillet over a moderate heat.
6. Add the remaining ingredients and simmer them, until the sauce has thickened and reduced slightly.
7. When done, serve the cube steak and drizzle the Cowboy sauce on the top.
8. Serve and enjoy.

Rosemary Ribeye Steaks

Servings: 2
Cooking Time: 15 Minutes
Ingredients:
- ¼ cup butter
- 1 clove garlic, minced
- Salt and ground black pepper, to taste
- 1½ tablespoons balsamic vinegar
- ¼ cup rosemary, chopped
- 2 ribeye steaks

Directions:
1. Melt the butter in a skillet over medium heat. Add the garlic and fry until fragrant.
2. Remove the skillet from the heat and add the salt, pepper, and vinegar. Allow it to cool.
3. Add the rosemary, then pour the mixture into a Ziploc bag.
4. Put the ribeye steaks in the bag and shake well, coating the meat well. Refrigerate for an hour, then allow to sit for a further twenty minutes.
5. Preheat the air fryer to 400°F (204°C) and set the rack inside. Air fry the ribeyes for 15 minutes.
6. Take care when removing the steaks from the air fryer and plate up.
7. Serve immediately.

Thyme Beef Roast

Servings: 7
Cooking Time: 35 Minutes
Ingredients:
- 2 pounds' beef roast
- 1 tablespoon olive oil
- 1 teaspoon thyme
- 2 teaspoons garlic powder
- ¼ teaspoon black pepper
- 1 tablespoon kosher salt

Directions:
1. Coat roast with olive oil.
2. Mix together thyme, garlic powder, black pepper, and salt and rub all over roast.
3. Place roast into the air fryer basket and cook at almost 400 degrees F/ 205 degrees C for 20 minutes.
4. Spray roast with cooking spray and cook for 15 minutes more.
5. Slice and serve.

Sizzling Beef Fajitas

Servings: 4
Cooking Time: 10 Minutes
Ingredients:
- 1 pound beef flank steak, cut into strips
- 1 red bell pepper, cut into strips
- 1 green bell pepper, cut into strips
- ½ red onion, cut into strips
- 2 tablespoons taco or fajita seasoning
- Salt
- Pepper
- 2 tablespoons extra-virgin olive oil
- 8 medium (8-inch) flour tortillas

Directions:
1. In a large bowl, combine the beef, red and green bell peppers, onion, taco seasoning, salt and pepper to taste, and olive oil. Mix well.
2. Transfer the beef and vegetable mixture to the air fryer. It is okay to stack. Cook for 5 minutes.
3. Open the air fryer and shake the basket. Cook for an additional 4 to 5 minutes.
4. Divide the beef and vegetables evenly among the tortillas and serve with any of your desired additional toppings.

Cajun Seasoned Bratwurst With Vegetables

Servings: 6
Cooking Time: 20 Minutes
Ingredients:
- 1 package bratwurst, sliced ½-inch rounds
- ½ tablespoon Cajun seasoning
- ¼ cup onion, diced
- 2 bell pepper, sliced

Directions:
1. Add all the recipe ingredients into the suitable mixing bowl and toss well.
2. Line air fryer basket with foil.
3. Add vegetable and bratwurst mixture into the air fryer basket and cook at almost 390 degrees F/ 200 degrees C for almost 10 minutes.
4. Toss well and cook for almost 10 minutes more.
5. Serve and enjoy.

Italian-style Cheeseburgers With Cheese Slices

Servings: 4
Cooking Time: 12 Minutes
Ingredients:
- 1-pound ground beef
- 4 cheddar cheese slices
- ½ teaspoon Italian seasoning
- Black pepper
- Salt

Directions:
1. Grease its air fryer basket with cooking spray.
2. In a suitable bowl, mix together ground beef, Italian seasoning, black pepper, and salt.
3. Make 4 equal shapes of patties from meat mixture and place into the air fryer basket.
4. Cook at almost 375 degrees F/ 190 degrees C for 5 minutes. Turn patties to another side and cook for 5 minutes more.
5. Place cheese slices on top of each patty and cook for 2 minutes more.
6. Serve and enjoy.

Sweet-and-sour Polish Sausage

Servings: 4
Cooking Time: 10 To 15 Minutes
Ingredients:
- ¾ pound Polish sausage
- 1 red bell pepper, cut into 1-inch strips
- ½ cup minced onion
- 3 tablespoons brown sugar
- ⅓ cup ketchup
- 2 tablespoons mustard
- 2 tablespoons apple cider vinegar
- ½ cup chicken broth

Directions:
1. Cut the sausage into 1½-inch pieces and put into a 6-inch metal bowl. Add the pepper and minced onion.
2. In a small bowl, combine the brown sugar, ketchup, mustard, apple cider vinegar, and chicken broth, and mix well. Pour into the bowl.
3. Roast for 10 to 15 minutes or until the sausage is hot, the vegetables tender, and the sauce bubbling and slightly thickened.
4. Did You Know? Polish sausage is almost always fully cooked when it is sold; read the label carefully to make sure you buy a fully cooked type for this recipe. Uncooked sausages are too fatty and release too much grease to cook in this appliance.

Air Fried Beef Ribs

Servings: 4
Cooking Time: 8 Minutes
Ingredients:
- 1 pound (454 g) meaty beef ribs, rinsed and drained
- 3 tablespoons apple cider vinegar
- 1 cup coriander, finely chopped
- 1 tablespoon fresh basil leaves, chopped
- 2 garlic cloves, finely chopped
- 1 chipotle powder
- 1 teaspoon fennel seeds
- 1 teaspoon hot paprika
- Kosher salt and black pepper, to taste
- ½ cup vegetable oil

Directions:
1. Coat the ribs with the remaining ingredients and refrigerate for at least 3 hours.
2. Preheat the air fryer to 360°F (182°C).
3. Separate the ribs from the marinade and put them on a grill pan. Air fry for 8 minutes.
4. Pour the remaining marinade over the ribs before serving.

Simple Rib-eye Steak

Servings: 2
Cooking Time: 14 Minutes
Ingredients:
- 2 medium-sized rib eye steaks
- Salt & freshly ground black pepper, to taste

Directions:
1. Use the kitchen towels to pat dry the steaks.
2. Season the rib eye steaks with salt and pepper well on both sides.
3. Cook the steaks at 400 degrees F/ 205 degrees C for 14 minutes, flipping halfway through.
4. Let the steaks cool for 5 minutes before serving.

Roast Beef And Brown Rice

Servings: 4
Cooking Time: 20 Minutes
Ingredients:
- 1 cup cooked brown rice
- 1 onion, chopped
- ½ cup carrot, grated
- 4 bell peppers, tops removed
- 2 teaspoons olive oil
- 2 medium beefsteak tomatoes, chopped
- 1 cup chopped cooked roast beef
- 1 teaspoon dried marjoram

Directions:
1. In a 6-by-2-inch pan, toss the chopped bell pepper tops, carrot, onion, and olive oil.
2. Cook for almost 4 minutes, or until the vegetables are crisp-tender.
3. Transfer the vegetables to a suitable bowl.
4. Add the brown rice, tomatoes, roast beef, and marjoram and mix.
5. Stuff the vegetable mixture into the hollow bell peppers.
6. Place the stuffed bell peppers in the air fryer basket.
7. Air fry for almost 16 minutes.
8. Serve immediately.

Vegetable Beef Meatballs With Herbs

Servings: 4
Cooking Time: 17 Minutes
Ingredients:
- 1 medium onion, minced
- 2 garlic cloves, minced
- 1 teaspoon olive oil
- 1 slice whole-wheat bread, crumbled
- 3 tablespoons (1 percent) milk
- 1 teaspoon dried marjoram
- 1 teaspoon dried basil
- 1-pound (96 percent) lean ground beef

Directions:
1. In a 6-by-2-inch pan, combine the onion, garlic, and olive oil.
2. Air-fry for 2 to 4 minutes, or until the vegetables are crisp-tender.
3. Transfer the vegetables to a suitable bowl, and add the bread crumbs, milk, marjoram, and basil. Mix well.
4. Add the ground beef.
5. With your hands, work the mixture gently but thoroughly until combined.
6. Form the meat mixture into about 24 1-inch meatballs.
7. Air fry the meatballs in the preheated Air Fryer basket for 12 to 17 minutes.
8. Serve immediately.

Beef Chuck With Brussels Sprouts

Servings: 4
Cooking Time: 15 Minutes
Ingredients:
- 1 pound (454 g) beef chuck shoulder steak
- 2 tablespoons vegetable oil
- 1 tablespoon red wine vinegar
- 1 teaspoon fine sea salt
- ½ teaspoon ground black pepper
- 1 teaspoon smoked paprika
- 1 teaspoon onion powder
- ½ teaspoon garlic powder
- ½ pound (227 g) Brussels sprouts, cleaned and halved
- ½ teaspoon fennel seeds
- 1 teaspoon dried basil
- 1 teaspoon dried sage

Directions:
1. Massage the beef with the vegetable oil, wine vinegar, salt, black pepper, paprika, onion powder, and garlic powder, coating it well.
2. Allow to marinate for a minimum of 3 hours.
3. Preheat the air fryer to 390°F (199°C).
4. Remove the beef from the marinade and put in the preheated air fryer. Air fry for 10 minutes. Flip the beef halfway through.
5. Put the prepared Brussels sprouts in the air fryer along with the fennel seeds, basil, and sage.
6. Lower the heat to 380°F (193°C) and air fry everything for another 5 minutes.
7. Give them a good stir. Air fry for an additional 10 minutes.
8. Serve immediately.

Stir-fried Steak And Cabbage

Servings: 4
Cooking Time: 8 To 13 Minutes
Ingredients:
- ½ pound sirloin steak, cut into strips
- 2 teaspoons cornstarch
- 1 tablespoon peanut oil
- 2 cups chopped red or green cabbage
- 1 yellow bell pepper, chopped
- 2 green onions, chopped
- 2 cloves garlic, sliced
- ½ cup commercial stir-fry sauce

Directions:
1. Toss the steak with the cornstarch and set aside.
2. In a 6-inch metal bowl, combine the peanut oil with the cabbage. Place in the basket and cook for 3 to 4 minutes.
3. Remove the bowl from the basket and add the steak, pepper, onions, and garlic. Return to the air fryer and cook for 3 to 5 minutes or until the steak is cooked to desired doneness and vegetables are crisp and tender.
4. Add the stir-fry sauce and cook for 2 to 4 minutes or until hot. Serve over rice.

Tasty Pork Chops

Servings: 4
Cooking Time: 9 Minutes
Ingredients:
- 4 pork chops, boneless
- 1 teaspoon onion powder
- 1 teaspoon smoked paprika
- ½ cup parmesan cheese, grated
- 2 tablespoons olive oil
- ½ teaspoon black pepper
- 1 teaspoon kosher salt

Directions:
1. Brush pork chops with olive oil.
2. In a suitable bowl, mix together parmesan cheese and spices.
3. Grease its air fryer basket with cooking spray.
4. Coat pork chops with parmesan cheese mixture and place in the air fryer basket.
5. Cook pork chops at 375 degrees F/ 190 degrees C for 9 minutes. Turn halfway through the cooking time.
6. Serve and enjoy.

Asian Sirloin Steaks With Worcestershire Sauce

Servings: 2
Cooking Time: 25 Minutes
Ingredients:
- 12 oz. sirloin steaks
- 1 tablespoon garlic, minced
- 1 tablespoon ginger, grated
- ½ tablespoon Worcestershire sauce
- 1 ½ tablespoon soy sauce
- 2 tablespoons Erythritol
- Black pepper
- Salt

Directions:
1. Add steaks in a large zip-lock bag along with remaining ingredients. Shake well and place in the refrigerator for overnight.
2. Spray its air fryer basket with cooking spray.
3. Place marinated steaks in air fryer basket and cook at almost 400 degrees F/ 205 degrees C for 10 minutes.
4. Turn steaks to another side and cook for 10-15 minutes more.
5. Serve and enjoy.

Montreal Steak

Servings: 2
Cooking Time: 7 Minutes
Ingredients:
- 12 oz. steak
- ½-teaspoon liquid smoke
- 1 tablespoon soy sauce
- ½-tablespoon cocoa powder
- 1 tablespoon Montreal steak seasoning
- Pepper
- Salt

Directions:
1. In a large zip-lock bag, coat the steak well with the liquid smoke, soy sauce, and steak seasonings, then refrigerate the mixture for overnight.
2. Coat the cooking basket of your air fryer with cooking spray.
3. Arrange the marinated steak to the air fryer and cook at 375 degrees F/ 190 degrees C for 7 minutes.
4. After that, turn the steak and cook another side for 5 minutes more.
5. Serve and enjoy.

Sumptuous Pizza Tortilla Rolls

Servings: 4
Cooking Time: 6 Minutes
Ingredients:
- 1 teaspoon butter
- ½ medium onion, slivered
- ½ red or green bell pepper, julienned
- 4 ounces (113 g) fresh white mushrooms, chopped
- ½ cup pizza sauce
- 8 flour tortillas
- 8 thin slices deli ham
- 24 pepperoni slices
- 1 cup shredded Mozzarella cheese
- Cooking spray

Directions:
1. Preheat the air fryer to 390°F (199°C).
2. Put butter, onions, bell pepper, and mushrooms in a baking pan. Bake in the preheated air fryer for 3 minutes. Stir and cook 3 to 4 minutes longer until just crisp and tender. Remove pan and set aside.
3. To assemble rolls, spread about 2 teaspoons of pizza sauce on one half of each tortilla. Top with a slice of ham and 3 slices of pepperoni. Divide sautéed vegetables among tortillas and top with cheese.
4. Roll up tortillas, secure with toothpicks if needed, and spray with oil.
5. Put 4 rolls in air fryer basket and air fry for 4 minutes. Turn and air fry 4 minutes, until heated through and lightly browned.
6. Repeat step 4 to air fry remaining pizza rolls.
7. Serve immediately.

Potato And Prosciutto Salad

Servings: 8
Cooking Time: 7 Minutes
Ingredients:
- Salad:
- 4 pounds (1.8 kg) potatoes, boiled and cubed
- 15 slices prosciutto, diced
- 2 cups shredded Cheddar cheese
- Dressing:
- 15 ounces (425 g) sour cream
- 2 tablespoons mayonnaise
- 1 teaspoon salt
- 1 teaspoon black pepper
- 1 teaspoon dried basil

Directions:
1. Preheat the air fryer to 350°F (177°C).
2. Put the potatoes, prosciutto, and Cheddar in a baking dish. Put it in the air fryer and air fry for 7 minutes.
3. In a separate bowl, mix the sour cream, mayonnaise, salt, pepper, and basil using a whisk.
4. Coat the salad with the dressing and serve.

Delectable Pork Chops

Servings: 2
Cooking Time: 12 Minutes
Ingredients:
- ½ lb. pork chops, boneless
- 4 tablespoons Swerve
- ½-teaspoon steak seasoning blend
- ½-tablespoon mustard

Directions:
1. Mix up the Swerve, steak seasoning blend and mustard in a small bowl, then rub the steak with the spice mixture.
2. Transfer the coated steak to the cooking basket in the air fryer and cook at 350 degrees F/ 175 degrees C for 12 minutes. flipping halfway through.
3. When done, serve and enjoy.

Steak And Vegetable Skewers

Servings: 4
Cooking Time: 7 Minutes
Ingredients:
- 2 tablespoons balsamic vinegar
- 2 teaspoons olive oil
- ½ teaspoon dried marjoram
- ⅛ teaspoon freshly black pepper
- ¾ pound round steak, cut into 1-inch pieces
- 1 red bell pepper, sliced
- 16 button mushrooms
- 1 cup cherry tomatoes

Directions:
1. In a suitable bowl, stir together the balsamic vinegar, olive oil, marjoram, and black pepper.
2. Add the steak and stir to coat. Let stand for almost 10 minutes at room temperature.
3. Alternating items, thread the beef, red bell pepper, mushrooms, and tomatoes onto 8 bamboo or metal skewers that fit in the air fryer.
4. Air fry in the preheated Air Fryer for 5 to 7 minutes, or until the beef is browned and reaches at least 145 degrees F/ 60 degrees C on a meat thermometer.
5. Serve immediately.

Sweet And Spicy Pork Chops

Servings: 4
Cooking Time: 15 Minutes
Ingredients:
- 1 tablespoon olive oil, plus more for spraying
- 3 tablespoons brown sugar
- ½ teaspoon cayenne pepper
- ½ teaspoon garlic powder
- ½ teaspoon salt
- ¼ teaspoon freshly ground black pepper
- 4 thin boneless pork chops, trimmed of excess fat

Directions:
1. Spray a fryer basket lightly with olive oil.
2. In a small bowl, mix together the brown sugar, 1 tablespoon of olive oil, cayenne pepper, garlic powder, salt, and black pepper.
3. Coat each pork chop with the marinade, shaking them to remove any excess, and place in the fryer basket in a single layer. You may need to cook them in batches.
4. Air fry for 7 minutes. Flip the pork chops over and brush with more marinade. Cook until the chops reach an internal temperature of 145°F, an additional 5 to 8 minutes.

Sausage, Peppers, And Onions

Servings: 5
Cooking Time: 15 Minutes
Ingredients:
- 5 Italian sausages
- 1 green bell pepper, seeded and cut into strips
- 1 red bell pepper, seeded and cut into strips
- ½ onion, cut into strips
- 1 teaspoon dried oregano
- ½ teaspoon garlic powder
- 5 Italian rolls or buns

Directions:
1. Place the sausages in the air fryer. No cooking oil is needed as the sausages will produce oil during the cooking process. The sausages should fit in the basket without stacking. If not, stacking is okay. Cook for 10 minutes.
2. Season the green and red bell peppers and the onion with the oregano and garlic powder.
3. Open the air fryer and flip the sausages. Add the peppers and onion to the basket. Cook for an additional 3 to 5 minutes, until the vegetables are soft and the sausages are no longer pink on the inside.
4. Serve the sausages (sliced or whole) on buns with the peppers and onion.

Cheese Ground Pork

Servings: 4
Cooking Time: 40 Minutes
Ingredients:
- 1 tablespoon olive oil
- 1 ½ pounds pork, ground
- Salt and black pepper, to taste
- 1 medium-sized leek, sliced
- 1 teaspoon fresh garlic, minced
- 2 carrots, trimmed and sliced
- 1 (2-ounce) jar pimiento, drained and chopped
- 1 can (10 ¾-ounces) condensed cream of mushroom soup
- 1 cup water
- ½ cup ale
- 1 cup cream cheese
- ½ cup soft fresh breadcrumbs
- 1 tablespoon fresh cilantro, chopped

Directions:
1. At 320 degrees F/ 160 degrees C, preheat your Air Fryer.
2. Spread the olive oil in a suitable baking dish and heat for 1 to 2 minutes.
3. Add the pork, salt, black pepper and cook for 6 minutes, crumbling with a fork.
4. Then stir in the leeks and cook for 4 to 5 minutes, with occasional stirring.
5. Add the garlic, carrots, pimiento, mushroom soup, water, ale, and cream cheese.
6. Gently stir to combine.
7. Turn the temperature to 370 degrees F/ 185 degrees C.
8. Top with the breadcrumbs.
9. Place the stuffed baking dish in the cooking basket and cook approximately 30 minutes or until everything is thoroughly cooked.
10. Serve garnished with fresh cilantro.

Simple Pork Chops

Servings: 3
Cooking Time: 12 Minutes
Ingredients:
- 3 boneless pork chops
- Salt and pepper, to taste
- ½ cup all-purpose flour
- ½ cup breadcrumbs
- 1 tablespoon honey
- 2 tablespoons olive oil
- 1 tablespoon Dijon mustard
- 1 tablespoon soy sauce

Directions:
1. In a zip-lock bag, mix up the soy sauce, honey, olive oil, Dijon mustard and pork chops, then seal and refrigerate for 30 minutes.
2. After remove the pork chops from the marinade, season them with salt, pepper and coat them with flour and breadcrumbs.
3. Cook the pork chops in your air fryer at 370 degrees F/ 185 degrees C for 12 minutes.
4. When done, serve and enjoy.

Unstuffed Cabbage

Servings:4
Cooking Time: 14 To 20 Minutes
Ingredients:
- 1 tablespoon olive oil
- 1 small onion, chopped
- 1½ cups chopped green cabbage
- 16 precooked frozen meatballs
- 1 cup frozen cooked rice
- 2 tomatoes, chopped
- ½ teaspoon dried marjoram
- Pinch salt
- Freshly ground black pepper

Directions:
1. In a 6-inch metal bowl, combine the oil and the onion. Bake for 2 to 4 minutes or until the onion is crisp and tender.
2. Add the cabbage, meatballs, rice, tomatoes, marjoram, salt, and pepper, and stir.
3. Bake for 12 to 16 minutes, stirring once during cooking time, until the meatballs are hot, the rice is warmed, and the vegetables are tender.

Orange Pork Tenderloin

Servings:4
Cooking Time: 23 Minutes
Ingredients:
- 2 tablespoons brown sugar
- 2 teaspoons cornstarch
- 2 teaspoons Dijon mustard
- ½ cup orange juice
- ½ teaspoon soy sauce
- 2 teaspoons grated fresh ginger
- ¼ cup white wine
- Zest of 1 orange
- 1 pound (454 g) pork tenderloin
- Salt and freshly ground black pepper, to taste
- Oranges, halved, for garnish
- Fresh parsley, for garnish

Directions:
1. Combine the brown sugar, cornstarch, Dijon mustard, orange juice, soy sauce, ginger, white wine and orange zest in a small saucepan and bring the mixture to a boil on the stovetop. Lower the heat and simmer while you air fry the pork tenderloin or until the sauce has thickened.
2. Preheat the air fryer to 370°F (188°C).
3. Season all sides of the pork tenderloin with salt and freshly ground black pepper. Transfer the tenderloin to the air fryer basket.
4. Air fry for 20 to 23 minutes, or until the internal temperature reaches 145°F (63°C). Flip the tenderloin over halfway through the cooking process and baste with the sauce.
5. Transfer the tenderloin to a cutting board and let it rest for 5 minutes. Slice the pork at a slight angle and serve immediately with orange halves and fresh parsley.
6. Serve immediately.

Ritzy Skirt Steak Fajitas

Servings: 4
Cooking Time: 30 Minutes
Ingredients:
- 2 tablespoons olive oil
- ¼ cup lime juice
- 1 clove garlic, minced
- ½ teaspoon ground cumin
- ½ teaspoon hot sauce
- ½ teaspoon salt
- 2 tablespoons chopped fresh cilantro
- 1 pound (454 g) skirt steak
- 1 onion, sliced
- 1 teaspoon chili powder
- 1 red pepper, sliced
- 1 green pepper, sliced
- Salt and freshly ground black pepper, to taste
- 8 flour tortillas
- Toppings:
- Shredded lettuce
- Crumbled Queso Fresco (or grated Cheddar cheese)
- Sliced black olives
- Diced tomatoes
- Sour cream
- Guacamole

Directions:
1. Combine the olive oil, lime juice, garlic, cumin, hot sauce, salt and cilantro in a shallow dish. Add the skirt steak and turn it over several times to coat all sides. Pierce the steak with a needle-style meat tenderizer or paring knife. Marinate the steak in the refrigerator for at least 3 hours, or overnight. When you are ready to cook, remove the steak from the refrigerator and let it sit at room temperature for 30 minutes.
2. Preheat the air fryer to 400°F (204°C).
3. Toss the onion slices with the chili powder and a little olive oil and transfer them to the air fryer basket. Air fry for 5 minutes. Add the red and green peppers to the air fryer basket with the onions, season with salt and pepper and air fry for 8 more minutes, until the onions and peppers are soft. Transfer the vegetables to a dish and cover with aluminum foil to keep warm.
4. Put the skirt steak in the air fryer basket and pour the marinade over the top. Air fry at 400°F (204°C) for 12 minutes. Flip the steak over and air fry for an additional 5 minutes. Transfer the cooked steak to a cutting board and let the steak rest for a few minutes. If the peppers and onions need to be heated, return them to the air fryer for just 1 to 2 minutes.
5. Thinly slice the steak at an angle, cutting against the grain of the steak. Serve the steak with the onions and peppers, the warm tortillas and the fajita toppings on the side.
6. Serve immediately.

Pork Cutlets

Servings: 2
Cooking Time: 1 Hour 20 Minutes
Ingredients:
- 1 cup water
- 1 cup red wine
- 1 tablespoon sea salt
- 2 pork cutlets
- ½ cup all-purpose flour
- ½ teaspoon shallot powder
- ½-teaspoon porcini powder
- Sea salt, to taste
- Ground black pepper, to taste
- 1 egg
- ¼ cup yogurt
- 1 teaspoon brown mustard
- 1 cup tortilla chips, crushed

Directions:
1. In a large ceramic dish, combine the water, wine and salt. After adding the pork cutlets, refrigerating the mixture for 1 hour.
2. In a shallow bowl, mix the flour, shallot powder, porcini powder, salt, and ground pepper.
3. In another bowl, whisk the eggs with yogurt and mustard.
4. In the third bowl, place the crushed tortilla chips.
5. Evenly coat the pork cutlets with the flour mixture and egg mixture in order, then, roll them over the crushed tortilla chips.
6. Lightly grease the bottom of the cooking basket with cooking oil.
7. Place the breaded pork cutlets on the basket and cook them at 395 degrees F/ 200 degrees C and for 10 minutes.
8. Flip and cook for 5 minutes more on the other side.
9. Serve warm.

Simple & Tasty Pork Sandwiches

Servings: 3
Cooking Time: 50 Minutes
Ingredients:
- 2 teaspoons. peanut oil
- 1 ½ pounds pork sirloin
- Coarse salt and black pepper, to taste
- 1 tablespoon smoked paprika
- ¼ cup prepared barbecue sauce
- 3 hamburger buns, split

Directions:
1. At 360 degrees F/ 180 degrees C, preheat your Air Fryer.
2. Drizzle the oil all over the pork sirloin.
3. Sprinkle with salt, black pepper, and paprika.
4. Cook for 50 minutes in the preheated Air Fryer.
5. Remove the prepared roast from the Air Fryer and shred with 2 forks.
6. Mix in the barbecue sauce.
7. Serve over hamburger buns.
8. Enjoy!

Fish And Seafood Recipes

Awesome Parmesan Shrimp

Servings: 6
Cooking Time: 10 Minutes
Ingredients:
- 2 pounds cooked shrimp, peeled and deveined
- 2 tablespoons olive oil
- ½ teaspoon onion powder
- 1 teaspoon basil
- ½ teaspoon oregano
- 2/3 cup parmesan cheese, grated
- 3 garlic cloves, minced
- ¼ teaspoon black pepper

Directions:
1. In a suitable mixing bowl, combine together garlic, oil, onion powder, oregano, black pepper, and cheese.
2. Add shrimp in a suitable bowl and toss until well coated.
3. Grease its air fryer basket with cooking spray.
4. Add shrimp into the air fryer basket and cook at almost 350 degrees F/ 175 degrees C for 8-10 minutes.
5. Serve and enjoy.

Tex-mex Salmon Stir-fry

Servings: 4
Cooking Time: 9 To 14 Minutes
Ingredients:
- 12 ounces salmon fillets, cut into 1½-inch cubes (see Tip)
- 1 red bell pepper, chopped
- 1 red onion, chopped
- 1 jalapeño pepper, minced
- ¼ cup low-sodium salsa
- 2 tablespoons low-sodium tomato juice
- 2 teaspoons peanut oil or safflower oil
- 1 teaspoon chili powder
- Brown rice or polenta, cooked (optional)

Directions:
1. In a medium metal bowl, stir together the salmon, red bell pepper, red onion, jalapeño, salsa, tomato juice, peanut oil, and chili powder.
2. Place the bowl in the air fryer and cook for 9 to 14 minutes, until the salmon is just cooked through and firm and the vegetables are crisp-tender, stirring once. Serve immediately over hot cooked brown rice or polenta, if desired.

Cajun Lemon Branzino

Servings: 4
Cooking Time: 8 Minutes
Ingredients:
- 1-pound branzino, trimmed, washed
- 1 teaspoon Cajun seasoning
- 1 tablespoon sesame oil
- 1 tablespoon lemon juice
- 1 teaspoon salt

Directions:
1. Carefully coat the branzino with salt and Cajun seasoning.
2. Drizzle the lemon juice and sesame oil over the branzino.
3. At 380 degrees F/ 195 degrees C, heat your air fryer in advance.
4. Place the branzino in the air fryer and cook it for 8 minutes at 380 degrees F/ 195 degrees C.
5. When done, serve and enjoy.

Zesty Garlic Scallops

Servings:4
Cooking Time: 15 Minutes
Ingredients:
- 2 teaspoons olive oil, plus more for spraying
- 1 packet dry zesty Italian dressing mix
- 1 teaspoon minced garlic
- 16 ounces small scallops, thawed, patted dry

Directions:
1. Spray a fryer basket lightly with olive oil.
2. In a large zip-top plastic bag, combine the olive oil, Italian dressing mix, and garlic.
3. Add the scallops, seal the zip-top bag, and coat the scallops in the seasoning mixture.
4. Place the scallops in the fryer basket and lightly spray with olive oil.
5. Air fry for 5 minutes, shake the basket, and cook until the scallops reach an internal temperature of 120°F, for 5 to 10 more minutes.

Tuna Veggie Stir-fry

Servings:4
Cooking Time: 7 To 12 Minutes
Ingredients:
- 1 tablespoon olive oil
- 1 red bell pepper, chopped
- 1 cup green beans, cut into 2-inch pieces
- 1 onion, sliced
- 2 cloves garlic, sliced
- 2 tablespoons low-sodium soy sauce
- 1 tablespoon honey
- ½ pound fresh tuna, cubed

Directions:
1. In a 6-inch metal bowl, combine the olive oil, pepper, green beans, onion, and garlic.
2. Cook in the air fryer for 4 to 6 minutes, stirring once, until crisp and tender. Add soy sauce, honey, and tuna, and stir.
3. Cook for another 3 to 6 minutes, stirring once, until the tuna is cooked as desired. Tuna can be served rare or medium-rare, or you can cook it until well done.

Delicious Grouper Filets

Servings: 3
Cooking Time: 10 Minutes
Ingredients:
- 1 pound grouper filets
- ¼ teaspoon shallot powder
- ¼ teaspoon porcini powder
- 1 teaspoon fresh garlic, minced
- ½ teaspoon cayenne pepper
- ½ teaspoon hot paprika
- ¼ teaspoon oregano
- ½ teaspoon marjoram
- ½ teaspoon sage
- 1 tablespoon butter, melted
- Sea salt and black pepper, to taste

Directions:
1. Use the kitchen towels to pat dry the grouper filets.
2. Mix up the remaining ingredients until well incorporated, then rub the grouper filets on all sides with the mixture.
3. Cook the grouper filets in the preheated Air Fryer at 400 degrees F/ 205 degrees C for 10 minutes, flipping halfway through.
4. Serve over hot rice if desired. Bon appétit!

Ginger Salmon Fillet

Servings: 4
Cooking Time: 22 Minutes
Ingredients:
- 2 salmon fillets
- 60g cane sugar
- 4 tablespoons soy sauce
- 50g sesame seeds
- Unlimited Ginger

Directions:
1. Preheat the air fryer at about 360 degrees F/ 180 degrees C for 5 minutes.
2. Put the sugar and soy sauce in the basket.
3. Cook everything for 5 minutes.
4. In the meantime, wash the fish well, pass it through sesame to cover it completely and place it inside the tank and add the fresh ginger.
5. Cook for 12 minutes.
6. Flip the salmon fillets and finish cooking for another 8 minutes.

Fish And Vegetable Tacos

Servings: 4
Cooking Time: 9 To 12 Minutes
Ingredients:
- 1 pound white fish fillets, such as sole or cod (see Tip)
- 2 teaspoons olive oil
- 3 tablespoons freshly squeezed lemon juice, divided
- 1½ cups chopped red cabbage
- 1 large carrot, grated
- ½ cup low-sodium salsa
- ⅓ cup low-fat Greek yogurt
- 4 soft low-sodium whole-wheat tortillas

Directions:
1. Brush the fish with the olive oil and sprinkle with 1 tablespoon of lemon juice. Air-fry in the air fryer basket for 9 to 12 minutes, or until the fish just flakes when tested with a fork.
2. Meanwhile, in a medium bowl, stir together the remaining 2 tablespoons of lemon juice, the red cabbage, carrot, salsa, and yogurt.
3. When the fish is cooked, remove it from the air fryer basket and break it up into large pieces.
4. Offer the fish, tortillas, and the cabbage mixture, and let each person assemble a taco.

Pancetta-wrapped Scallops With Pancetta Slices

Servings: 3
Cooking Time: 10 Minutes
Ingredients:
- 1 pound sea scallops
- 1 tablespoon deli mustard
- 2 tablespoons soy sauce
- ¼ teaspoon shallot powder
- ¼ teaspoon garlic powder
- ½ teaspoon dried dill
- Sea salt, to taste
- Ground black pepper, to taste
- 4 ounces' pancetta slices

Directions:
1. Transfer the sea scallops that have patted dry in advance to a mixing bowl, the add the deli mustard, soy sauce, shallot powder, garlic powder, dill, salt, black pepper and toss well.
2. Use a bacon slice to wrap one scallop, when finished, transfer the scallop wraps to the cooking basket.
3. Cook the scallop wraps in your Air Fryer at 400 degrees F/ 205 degrees C for 7 minutes.
4. After 4 minutes of cooking time, turn them over and cook an additional 3 minutes.
5. Serve with hot sauce for dipping if desired. Bon appétit!

Easy Air Fried Salmon

Servings: 2
Cooking Time: 10 Minutes
Ingredients:
- 2 salmon fillets, skinless and boneless
- 1 teaspoon olive oil
- Black pepper
- Salt

Directions:
1. Coat boneless salmon fillets with olive oil and season with black pepper and salt.
2. Place salmon fillets in air fryer basket and Cook at almost 360 degrees F/ 180 degrees C for 8-10 minutes.
3. Serve and enjoy.

Creamy Tuna With Zucchinis

Servings: 4
Cooking Time: 20 Minutes
Ingredients:
- 4 medium zucchinis
- 120g of tuna in oil canned drained
- 30g grated cheese
- 1 teaspoon pine nuts
- Salt, black pepper to taste

Directions:
1. Cut the zucchini in ½ laterally and empty it with a small spoon set aside the pulp that will be used for filling; place them in the basket.
2. In a food processor, put the zucchini pulp, drained tuna, pine nuts and grated cheese.
3. Mix until you get a homogeneous and dense mixture.
4. Fill the zucchini. Set the air fryer to 360 degrees F/ 180 degrees C.
5. Air fry for almost 20 minutes depending on the size of the zucchini. Let cool before serving.

Garlic Scallops With Parsley

Servings: 4
Cooking Time: 10 Minutes
Ingredients:
- 1 cup bread crumbs
- ¼ cup chopped parsley
- 16 sea scallops, rinsed and drained
- 2 shallots, chopped
- 3 pinches ground nutmeg
- 1½ tablespoons olive oil
- 5 cloves garlic, minced
- 2 tablespoons butter, melted
- salt and pepper to taste

Directions:
1. Coat the baking pan that fits your air fryer with cooking spray lightly.
2. Mix in melted butter, shallots, garlic and scallops, then season with nutmeg, salt and pepper.
3. Whisk the olive oil and bread crumbs well in a small bowl, then sprinkle over the processed scallops.
4. Cook the scallops at 390 degrees F/ 200 degrees C for 10 minutes or until the tops are lightly browned.
5. Sprinkle the parsley, serve and enjoy.

Flavor Calamari With Mediterranean Sauce

Servings: 4
Cooking Time: 4 Minutes
Ingredients:
- ½ pound calamari tubes cut into rings, cleaned
- Sea salt, to taste
- Ground black pepper, to season
- ½ cup almond flour
- ½ cup all-purpose flour
- 4 tablespoons parmesan cheese, grated
- ½ cup ale beer
- ¼ teaspoon cayenne pepper
- ½ cup breadcrumbs
- ¼ cup mayonnaise
- ¼ cup Greek-style yogurt
- 1 clove garlic, minced
- 1 tablespoon fresh lemon juice
- 1 teaspoon fresh parsley, chopped
- 1 teaspoon fresh dill, chopped

Directions:
1. Sprinkle salt and black pepper on the calamari.
2. In a bowl, mix the flour, cheese and beer until well combined.
3. In another bowl, mix cayenne pepper and breadcrumbs.
4. Coat the calamari pieces with the flour mixture and then roll them onto the breadcrumb mixture, pressing to coat on all sides.
5. Lightly oil the cooking basket and transfer the calamari pieces in it.
6. Cook the calamari pieces at 400 degrees F/ 205 degrees C for 4 minutes, shaking the basket halfway through.
7. Meanwhile, thoroughly mix the remaining ingredients well.
8. Serve warm calamari with the sauce for dipping.
9. Enjoy!

Cajun Salmon Burgers

Servings: 4
Cooking Time: 15 Minutes
Ingredients:
- Olive oil
- 4 (5-ounce) cans pink salmon in water, any skin and bones removed, drained
- 2 eggs, beaten
- 1 cup whole-wheat bread crumbs
- 4 tablespoons light mayonnaise
- 2 teaspoons Cajun seasoning
- 2 teaspoons dry mustard
- 4 whole-wheat buns

Directions:
1. Spray a fryer basket lightly with olive oil.
2. In a medium bowl, mix together the salmon, egg, bread crumbs, mayonnaise, Cajun seasoning, and dry mustard. Cover with plastic wrap and refrigerate for 30 minutes.
3. Shape the mixture into four ½-inch-thick patties about the same size as the buns.
4. Place the salmon patties in the fryer basket in a single layer and lightly spray the tops with olive oil. You may need to cook them in batches.
5. Air fry for 6 to 8 minutes. Turn the patties over and lightly spray with olive oil. Cook until crispy on the outside, 4 to 7 more minutes.
6. Serve on whole-wheat buns.

Spicy Jumbo Shrimps

Servings: 4
Cooking Time: 6 Minutes
Ingredients:
- ¼-teaspoon cayenne pepper
- ¼-teaspoon red chili flakes
- 1 teaspoon cumin
- 1 teaspoon oregano
- 1 teaspoon salt
- 1 teaspoon thyme
- 1 tablespoon coconut oil
- 1 teaspoon cilantro
- 1 teaspoon onion powder
- 1 teaspoon smoked paprika
- 20 jumbo shrimps, peeled and deveined

Directions:
1. In addition to the shrimps, combine the other ingredients well and then coat the shrimps.
2. Place the shrimps on the cooking pan and arrange the pan to your air fryer.
3. Cook for 6 minutes at 390 degrees F/ 200 degrees C.
4. When done, serve and enjoy.

Mustard-crusted Fish Fillets

Servings: 4
Cooking Time: 8 To 11 Minutes
Ingredients:
- 5 teaspoons low-sodium yellow mustard (see Tip)
- 1 tablespoon freshly squeezed lemon juice
- 4 (3.5-ounce) sole fillets
- ½ teaspoon dried thyme
- ½ teaspoon dried marjoram
- ⅛ teaspoon freshly ground black pepper
- 1 slice low-sodium whole-wheat bread, crumbled
- 2 teaspoons olive oil

Directions:
1. In a small bowl, mix the mustard and lemon juice. Spread this evenly over the fillets. Place them in the air fryer basket.
2. In another small bowl, mix the thyme, marjoram, pepper, bread crumbs, and olive oil. Mix until combined.
3. Gently but firmly press the spice mixture onto the top of each fish fillet.
4. Bake for 8 to 11 minutes, or until the fish reaches an internal temperature of at least 145°F on a meat thermometer and the topping is browned and crisp. Serve immediately.

Healthy Cardamom Salmon

Servings: 2
Cooking Time: 12 Minutes
Ingredients:
- 2 salmon fillets
- 1 tablespoon olive oil
- ¼ teaspoon ground cardamom
- ½ teaspoon paprika
- Salt

Directions:
1. At 350 degrees F/ 175 degrees C, preheat your air fryer.
2. Coat salmon fillets with paprika, cardamom, olive oil, and salt and place into the air fryer basket.
3. Cook salmon for almost 10-12 minutes. Turn halfway through.
4. Serve and enjoy.

Pesto Fish Finger Sandwich

Servings: 4
Cooking Time: 15 Minutes
Ingredients:
- 4 finger fish fillets
- 2 tablespoons flour
- 10 capers
- 4 bread rolls
- 2 ounces breadcrumbs
- 4 tablespoons pesto sauce
- 4 lettuce leaves
- Black pepper and salt, to taste

Directions:
1. At 370 degrees F/ 185 degrees C, preheat your air fryer.
2. Season the finger fish fillets with black pepper and salt, and coat them with the dry flour first; then dip in the breadcrumbs.
3. Arrange the fillets onto a baking mat and cook in the air fryer for almost 10 to 15 minutes.
4. Cut the bread rolls in half.
5. Place a lettuce leaf on top of the bottom halves; put the fillets over.
6. Spread a tablespoon of pesto sauce on top of each fillet, and top with the remaining halves.
7. Serve.

Salmon Patty Bites

Servings:4
Cooking Time: 15 Minutes
Ingredients:
- Olive oil
- 4 (5-ounce) cans pink salmon, skinless, boneless in water, drained
- 2 eggs, beaten
- 1 cup whole-wheat panko bread crumbs
- 4 tablespoons finely minced red bell pepper
- 2 tablespoons parsley flakes
- 2 teaspoons Old Bay seasoning

Directions:
1. Spray a fryer basket lightly with olive oil.
2. In a medium bowl, mix together the salmon, eggs, panko bread crumbs, red bell pepper, parsley flakes, and Old Bay seasoning.
3. Using a small cookie scoop, form the mixture into 20 balls.
4. Place the salmon bites in the fryer basket in a single layer and spray lightly with olive oil. You may need to cook them in batches.
5. Air fry until crispy for 10 to 15 minutes, shaking the basket a couple of times for even cooking.

Beer Squid

Servings: 3
Cooking Time: 20 Minutes
Ingredients:
- 1 cup beer
- 1 lb. squid
- 1 cup all-purpose flour
- 2 eggs
- ½ cup cornstarch
- Sea salt, to taste
- ½-teaspoon ground black pepper
- 1 tablespoon Old Bay seasoning

Directions:
1. At 390 degrees F/ 200 degrees C, heat your air fryer in advance.
2. Clean the squid and then cut them into rings. Add the beer and squid in a glass bowl, cover and let it sit in your refrigerator for 1 hour.
3. Rinse the squid before patting it dry.
4. Add the flour in a shallow bowl; in another bowl, whisk the eggs. Lastly, in a third shallow bowl, add the cornstarch and seasonings.
5. Dredge the calamari in the flour.
6. Then dip the rings into the egg mixture and coat them with the cornstarch on all sided.
7. Arrange them in the cooking basket. Spritz with cooking oil and cook for 9 to 12 minutes, depending on the desired level of doneness. Work in batches.
8. Serve warm with your favorite dipping sauce. Enjoy!

Creamy Savory Salmon

Servings: 4
Cooking Time: 25 Minutes
Ingredients:
- For salmon:
- 2 teaspoons olive oil
- 24-ounce (4 pieces) salmon
- 1 pinch salt
- For the sauce:
- ½ cup sour cream
- ½ cup non-fat: Greek yogurt
- 1 pinch salt
- 2 tablespoons dill, finely chopped

Directions:
1. Make the salmon pieces of 6 ounces each, brush the pieces with olive oil and then top them with salt.
2. Place the pieces in the basket that has been coated with cooking oil or spray.
3. Arrange the basket to the air fryer and cook at 270 degrees F/ 130 degrees C for 20-25 minutes.
4. In a bowl of medium size, thoroughly mix the sauce ingredients.
5. When the pieces has finished, serve warm with the sauce!

Glazed Salmon With Soy Sauce

Servings: 2
Cooking Time: 14 Minutes
Ingredients:
- 1 teaspoon water
- 2 3½-ounce salmon fillets
- ⅓ cup soy sauce
- ⅓ cup honey
- 3 teaspoons rice wine vinegar

Directions:
1. At 355 degrees F/ 180 degrees C, preheat your air fryer. and grease an air fryer grill pan.
2. Mix all the recipe ingredients in a suitable bowl except salmon.
3. Reserve ½ of the mixture in a suitable bowl and coat the salmon in remaining mixture.
4. Refrigerate, covered for about 2 hours and place the salmon in the air fryer basket.
5. Cook for about 13 minutes, flipping once in between and coat with reserved marinade.
6. Place the leftover salmon marinade in a small pan and cook for about 1 minute.
7. Serve salmon with marinade sauce and enjoy.

Flounder Filets With Parmesan Cheese

Servings: 3
Cooking Time: 10 Minutes
Ingredients:
- 1 pound flounder filets
- 1 teaspoon garlic, minced
- 2 tablespoons soy sauce
- 1 teaspoon Dijon mustard
- ¼ cup malt vinegar
- 1 teaspoon granulated sugar
- Salt and black pepper, to taste
- ½ cup plain flour
- 1 egg
- 2 tablespoons milk
- ½ cup parmesan cheese, grated

Directions:
1. In a suitable bowl, combine the flounder filets with garlic, soy sauce, mustard, vinegar and sugar.
2. Marinate the flounder filets by refrigerating it for at least 1 hour.
3. When marinated, take the flounder filets out of the marinade and season with salt and pepper.
4. Place the plain flour in a suitable shallow bowl.
5. In another bowl, beat the egg and add milk until pale and well combined, then in the third bowl, place the Parmesan cheese.
6. Coat the flounder filet with the flour, egg mixture and Parmesan in order, pressing to adhere.
7. Coat the remaining flounder filets with the same steps.
8. Cook the flounder filets in the preheated Air Fryer at 400 degrees F/ 205 degrees C for 10 minutes, flipping halfway through.
9. When done, serve and enjoy.

Salmon Patties

Servings: 2 Servings
Cooking Time: 25 Minutes
Ingredients:
- 2 (7.5-oz) cans of unsalted pink salmon
- ½ cup of panko bread crumbs
- 1 large egg
- 2 tablespoons of mayonnaise
- 2 tablespoons of chopped fresh dill
- 2 teaspoons of mustard
- Lime wedges, for serving
- Pinch of black pepper and salt, to taste

Directions:
1. Preheat your air fryer to 400°F. Spray some oil inside the air fryer basket.
2. Drain water from the salmon, remove skin and large bones, put it in a medium bowl. Add in bread crumbs, mayonnaise, egg, mustard, pepper, and dill. Mix it well until combined. Form 4 same-sized patties.*
3. Put the patties in the air fryer basket in a single layer; avoid them touching. Cook at 400°F for 6 minutes, gently flip them, and cook for another 6 minutes until browned.
4. Serve warm with lemon wedges and enjoy your Salmon Patties!

Crab Cakes

Servings: 4 Servings
Cooking Time: 15 Minutes
Ingredients:
- 8 ounces of lump crab meat
- 3 chopped green onions
- 1 chopped red bell pepper
- 3 tablespoons of bread crumbs
- 3 tablespoons of mayonnaise
- 2 teaspoons of Old Bay seasoning
- 1 teaspoon of lemon juice
- Lemon wedges, for serving

Directions:
1. Preheat your air fryer to 370°F. Cover the inside of the air fryer basket with the perforated parchment paper.
2. Mix the crab meat, onions, bread crumbs, lemon juice, seasonings, pepper, and mayonnaise in a large bowl until well combined. Gently form same-sized patties.*
3. Transfer the formed patties in the preheated air fryer basket in a single layer. Cook at 370°F for 8–10 minutes until the crust is golden-brown.
4. Serve with your favorite sauce and lemon wedges. Enjoy your Crab Cakes!

Coconut Shrimp

Servings: 4
Cooking Time: 5 To 7 Minutes
Ingredients:
- 1 (8-ounce) can crushed pineapple
- ½ cup sour cream
- ¼ cup pineapple preserves
- 2 egg whites
- ⅔ cup cornstarch
- ⅔ cup sweetened coconut
- 1 cup panko bread crumbs
- 1 pound uncooked large shrimp, thawed if frozen, deveined and shelled
- Olive oil for misting

Directions:
1. Drain the crushed pineapple well, reserving the juice.
2. In a small bowl, combine the pineapple, sour cream, and preserves, and mix well. Set aside.
3. In a shallow bowl, beat the egg whites with 2 tablespoons of the reserved pineapple liquid. Place the cornstarch on a plate. Combine the coconut and bread crumbs on another plate.
4. Dip the shrimp into the cornstarch, shake it off, then dip into the egg white mixture and finally into the coconut mixture.
5. Place the shrimp in the air fryer basket and mist with oil. Air-fry for 5 to 7 minutes or until the shrimp are crisp and golden brown.
6. Did You Know? Shrimp are graded by how many there are in a pound. Large shrimp are usually 26 to 30 per pound, medium shrimp are 36 to 45 per pound. You can buy them shelled, deveined, and ready to cook, or fully cooked.

Cajun Fish Cakes

Servings: 4
Cooking Time: 30 Minutes
Ingredients:
- 2 catfish fillets
- 1 cup all-purpose flour
- 1 ounce butter
- 1 teaspoon baking powder
- 1 teaspoon baking soda
- ½ cup buttermilk
- 1 teaspoon Cajun seasoning
- 1 cup Swiss cheese, shredded

Directions:
1. Boil a pot of water, the put in the fish fillets and boil for 5 minutes or until it is opaque.
2. When done, flake the fish into small pieces.
3. In a bowl, mix up the other ingredients, then add the fish and mix them well.
4. Form 12 fish patties from the mixture.
5. Place the patties to the cooking pan and arrange the pan to your air fryer.
6. Cook at 380 degrees F/ 195 degrees C for 15 minutes.
7. Working in batches is suggested.
8. Enjoy!

Parsley Saltine Fillets

Servings: 4
Cooking Time: 12 Minutes
Ingredients:
- 1 cup crushed saltines
- ¼ cup extra-virgin olive oil
- 1 teaspoon garlic powder
- ½ teaspoon shallot powder
- 1 egg, well whisked
- 4 white fish fillets
- Salt and black pepper to taste
- Fresh Italian parsley to serve

Directions:
1. Combine the crushed saltines and olive oil in a suitable shallow bowl.
2. Mix together the garlic powder, shallot powder, and the beaten egg in a separate bowl.
3. Sprinkle a good amount of black pepper and salt over the fish, before dipping each fillet into the egg mixture.
4. Coat the fillets with the crumb mixture.
5. Air fry the fish at 370 degrees F/ 185 degrees C for almost 10 - 12 minutes.
6. Serve with fresh parsley.

Glazed Fillets

Servings: 4
Cooking Time: 15 Minutes
Ingredients:
- 4 flounder fillets
- 1 ½ tablespoons dark sesame oil
- 2 tablespoons sake
- Sea salt and cracked mixed peppercorns, as needed
- ¼ cup soy sauce
- 1 teaspoon brown sugar
- 1 tablespoon grated lemon rind
- 2 garlic cloves, minced
- Fresh chopped chives, to serve

Directions:
1. To marinate, prepare a large deep dish, add the ingredients except for chives and stir a little. Cover and refrigerate for 2-3 hours.
2. Add the fish to the basket that has been coated with the cooking oil or spray.
3. Arrange it to the air fryer and cook at 360 degrees F/ 180 degrees C for 12 minutes, flipping halfway through.
4. Pour the remaining marinade into a saucepan; simmer over medium-low heat until it has thickened.
5. Serve the fish with the marinade and chives on top!

Cajun Shrimp With Veggie

Servings: 4
Cooking Time: 20 Minutes
Ingredients:
- 50 small shrimp
- 1 tablespoon Cajun seasoning
- 1 bag of frozen mix vegetables
- 1 tablespoon olive oil

Directions:
1. Line air fryer basket with aluminum foil.
2. Add all the recipe ingredients into the suitable mixing bowl and toss well.
3. Transfer shrimp and vegetable mixture into the air fryer basket and cook at almost 350 degrees F/ 175 degrees C for almost 10 minutes.
4. Toss well and cook for almost 10 minutes more.
5. Serve and enjoy.

Quick Paella

Servings: 4
Cooking Time: 13 To 17 Minutes
Ingredients:
- 1 (10-ounce) package frozen cooked rice, thawed
- 1 (6-ounce) jar artichoke hearts, drained and chopped
- ¼ cup vegetable broth
- ½ teaspoon turmeric
- ½ teaspoon dried thyme
- 1 cup frozen cooked small shrimp
- ½ cup frozen baby peas
- 1 tomato, diced

Directions:
1. In a 6-by-6-by-2-inch pan, combine the rice, artichoke hearts, vegetable broth, turmeric, and thyme, and stir gently.
2. Place in the air fryer and bake for 8 to 9 minutes or until the rice is hot.
3. Remove from the air fryer and gently stir in the shrimp, peas, and tomato. Cook for 5 to 8 minutes or until the shrimp and peas are hot and the paella is bubbling.

Healthy Salmon With Cardamom

Servings: 2
Cooking Time: 12 Minutes
Ingredients:
- 2 salmon fillets
- 1 tablespoon olive oil
- ¼ teaspoon ground cardamom
- ½ teaspoon paprika
- Salt

Directions:
1. At 350 degrees F/ 175 degrees C, preheat your air fryer.
2. Coat salmon fillets with paprika, olive oil, cardamom, paprika, and salt and place into the air fryer basket.
3. Cook salmon for almost 10-12 minutes. Turn halfway through.
4. Serve and enjoy.

Lime Trout With Parsley

Servings: 4
Cooking Time: 12 Minutes
Ingredients:
- 4 trout fillets, boneless
- 4 tablespoons butter, melted
- Black pepper and salt to the taste
- Juice of 1 lime
- 1 tablespoon chives, chopped
- 1 tablespoon parsley, chopped

Directions:
1. Mix the fish fillets with the melted butter, black pepper and salt, rub gently, put the trout fillets in your air fryer basket and cook at almost 390 degrees F/ 200 degrees C for 6 minutes per side.
2. Divide between plates and serve with lime juice drizzled on top and with parsley and chives sprinkled at the end.

Asian Swordfish

Servings: 4
Cooking Time: 6 To 11 Minutes
Ingredients:
- 4 (4-ounce) swordfish steaks
- ½ teaspoon toasted sesame oil (see Tip)
- 1 jalapeño pepper, finely minced
- 2 garlic cloves, grated
- 1 tablespoon grated fresh ginger
- ½ teaspoon Chinese five-spice powder
- ⅛ teaspoon freshly ground black pepper
- 2 tablespoons freshly squeezed lemon juice

Directions:
1. Place the swordfish steaks on a work surface and drizzle with the sesame oil.
2. In a small bowl, mix the jalapeño, garlic, ginger, five-spice powder, pepper, and lemon juice. Rub this mixture into the fish and let it stand for 10 minutes.
3. Roast the swordfish in the air fryer for 6 to 11 minutes, or until the swordfish reaches an internal temperature of at least 140°F on a meat thermometer. Serve immediately.

Garlic Shrimp

Servings: 2 Servings
Cooking Time: 20 Minutes
Ingredients:
- 1 pound of peeled raw shrimp
- ¼ teaspoon of garlic powder
- Olive oil, to coat
- Pinch of salt, black pepper, and chili flakes, to taste
- Minced cilantro, for garnishing
- Lemon wedges, for serving

Directions:
1. Preheat your air fryer to 400°F.
2. Add the shrimp, garlic powder, oil, pepper, and salt to a mixing bowl. Mix it until all shrimp are coated. Transfer the shrimp in the preheated air fryer basket in a single layer.
3. Cook at 400°F for 10–14 minutes, stirring and flipping occasionally.
4. Serve warm with lemon wedges. Top with minced cilantro and chili flakes. Enjoy your Garlic Shrimp!

Crumbs Crusted Shrimp

Servings: 8
Cooking Time: 8 Minutes
Ingredients:
- 2-pound shrimp, peeled and deveined
- 4 egg whites
- 2 tablespoons olive oil
- 1 cup flour
- ½ teaspoon cayenne pepper
- 1 cup bread crumbs
- Black pepper and salt to taste

Directions:
1. Combine together the flour, black pepper, and salt in a shallow bowl.
2. In a separate bowl, mix the egg whites using a whisk.
3. In a third bowl, combine the bread crumbs, cayenne pepper, and salt.
4. At 400 degrees F/ 205 degrees C, preheat your air fryer.
5. Cover the shrimp with the flour mixture before dipping it in the egg white and lastly rolling in the bread crumbs.
6. Put the coated shrimp in the fryer's basket and top with a light drizzle of olive oil.
7. Air fry the shrimp at almost 400 degrees F/ 205 degrees C for 8 minutes, in multiple batches if necessary.

Cilantro-lime Fried Shrimp

Servings: 4
Cooking Time: 10 Minutes
Ingredients:
- 1 pound raw shrimp, peeled and deveined with tails on or off (see Prep tip)
- ½ cup chopped fresh cilantro
- Juice of 1 lime
- 1 egg
- ½ cup all-purpose flour
- ¾ cup bread crumbs
- Salt
- Pepper
- Cooking oil
- ½ cup cocktail sauce (optional)

Directions:
1. Place the shrimp in a plastic bag and add the cilantro and lime juice. Seal the bag. Shake to combine. Marinate in the refrigerator for 30 minutes.
2. In a small bowl, beat the egg. In another small bowl, place the flour. Place the bread crumbs in a third small bowl, and season with salt and pepper to taste.
3. Spray the air fryer basket with cooking oil.
4. Remove the shrimp from the plastic bag. Dip each in the flour, then the egg, and then the bread crumbs.
5. Place the shrimp in the air fryer. It is okay to stack them. Spray the shrimp with cooking oil. Cook for 4 minutes.
6. Open the air fryer and flip the shrimp. I recommend flipping individually instead of shaking to keep the breading intact. Cook for an additional 4 minutes, or until crisp.
7. Cool before serving. Serve with cocktail sauce if desired.

Typical Cod Nuggets

Servings: 4
Cooking Time: 10 Minutes
Ingredients:
- 16-ounce cod
- To make the breading:
- 1 cup all-purpose flour
- 2 tablespoons olive oil
- 2 eggs, beaten
- 1 pinch salt
- ¾ cup panko breadcrumbs, finely processed

Directions:
1. Thoroughly mix the oil, salt and crumbs in a medium-size bowl.
2. Take the cod, make pieces from it of about 5 inches by 1 inch.
3. In a bowl of medium size, thoroughly mix the salt, oil and crumbs.
4. Side by side place three bowls; add the flour in the first bowl, crumb mixture in the second and eggs in the third. Dip the fish in the flour, one by one, and then mix in the egg mix.
5. Lastly coat with the crumb mixture completely.
6. Place the fish pieces in the basket that has been coated with cooking oil or spray.
7. Arrange the basket to the air fryer and cook at 390 degrees F/ 200 degrees C for 10 minutes or until turn pink.
8. Serve the crispy fish!

Fish Mania With Mustard

Servings: 4-5
Cooking Time: 10 Minutes
Ingredients:
- 1 cup soft bread crumbs
- 1 teaspoon whole-grain mustard
- 2 cans canned fish
- 2 celery stalks, chopped
- 1 egg, whisked
- ½ teaspoon sea salt
- ¼ teaspoon black peppercorns, cracked
- 1 teaspoon paprika

Directions:
1. Thoroughly mix the fish, breadcrumbs, celery and other ingredients in a large bowl.
2. Make four cakes shapes from the mixture and refrigerate for 45-50 minutes.
3. Place the cakes in the basket that has been coated with cooking oil or spray.
4. Arrange it to air fryer and cook for 5 minutes at 360 degrees F/ 180 degrees C.
5. After 5 minutes, flip the cakes gently and cook for another 4 minutes
6. Serve over mashed potatoes.

Oregano Pollock With Capers

Servings: 3
Cooking Time: 13 Minutes
Ingredients:
- 2 tablespoons olive oil
- 1 red onion, sliced
- 2 garlic cloves, chopped
- 1 Florina pepper, deveined and minced
- 3 Pollock fillets, skinless
- 2 ripe tomatoes, diced
- 12 Kalamata olives, pitted and chopped
- 2 tablespoons capers
- 1 teaspoon oregano
- 1 teaspoon rosemary
- Salt, to taste
- ½ cup white wine

Directions:
1. At 360 degrees F/ 180 degrees C, preheat your air fryer. Heat the oil in a suitable baking pan.
2. Once hot, sauté the onion, garlic, and black pepper for 2 to 3 minutes or until fragrant.
3. Add the fish fillets to the baking pan.
4. Top with the tomatoes, olives, and capers. Sprinkle with the oregano, rosemary, and salt.
5. Pour in white wine and transfer to the cooking basket.
6. Turn the temperature to 395 degrees F/ 200 degrees C and air fry for almost 10 minutes.
7. Enjoy!

Tender Salmon

Servings: 4 Servings
Cooking Time: 30 Minutes
Ingredients:
- 4 salmon fillets
- 4 teaspoons of soy sauce
- 3 tablespoons of maple syrup
- 1 teaspoon of minced garlic
- 1/8 teaspoon of black pepper

Directions:
1. Add soy sauce, maple syrup, black pepper, and garlic to a bowl. Mix it until well combined. Put the salmon fillets in a Ziplock bag and pour in the prepared marinade. Leave it for 10–30 minutes for good flavor.
2. Preheat your air fryer to 350°F. Spray some oil inside the air fryer basket.
3. Transfer the marinated filets into the air fryer basket in a single layer.* Cook at 350°F for 8–10 minutes if you like medium-rare. Cook for 10–12 minutes, if you prefer well done.** The internal temperature for medium-rare should be 120–125°F, and for well-done will be 140°F.
4. Serve warm*** and enjoy your Tender Salmon!

Lemon Salmon With Chili

Servings: 4
Cooking Time: 17 Minutes
Ingredients:
- 2 pounds salmon fillet, skinless and boneless
- 2 lemon juice
- 1 orange juice
- 1 tablespoon olive oil
- 1 bunch fresh dill
- 1 chili, sliced
- Black pepper
- Salt

Directions:
1. At 325 degrees F/ 160 degrees C, preheat your air fryer.
2. Place salmon fillets in its air fryer basket.
3. Drizzle the salmon fillets with olive oil, lemon juice, and orange juice.
4. Sprinkle chili slices over salmon and season with black pepper and salt.
5. Place pan in the preheated air fryer and cook for almost 15-17 minutes.
6. Garnish with dill and serve.

Flavored Salmon Grill With Oregano & Cumin

Servings: 4
Cooking Time: 15 Minutes
Ingredients:
- 1 ½ lbs. skinless salmon fillet (preferably wild), cut into 1" pieces
- 1 teaspoon ground cumin
- 1 teaspoon kosher salt
- ¼-teaspoon crushed red pepper flakes
- 2 lemons, very thinly sliced into rounds
- 1 tablespoon chopped fresh oregano
- 1 tablespoon olive oil
- 1 teaspoon sesame seeds

Directions:
1. Prepare a small bowl, mix well oregano, sesame seeds, cumin, salt, and pepper flakes.
2. Thread salmon and folded lemon slices in a skewer.
3. Brush the salmon with oil and sprinkle with spice.
4. Arrange the skewers to the air fryer and cook for 5 minutes at 360 degrees F/ 180 degrees C.
5. Serve and enjoy.

Desserts And Sweets Recipes

Apple-peach Crisp

Servings: 4
Cooking Time:10 To 12 Minutes
Ingredients:
- 1 apple, peeled and chopped
- 2 peaches, peeled, pitted, and chopped
- 2 tablespoons honey
- ½ cup quick-cooking oatmeal
- ⅓ cup whole-wheat pastry flour
- 3 tablespoons packed brown sugar
- 2 tablespoons unsalted butter, at room temperature
- ½ teaspoon ground cinnamon

Directions:
1. In a 6-by-2-inch pan, thoroughly mix the apple, peaches, and honey.
2. In a medium bowl, stir together the oatmeal, pastry flour, brown sugar, butter, and cinnamon until crumbly. Sprinkle this mixture over the fruit.
3. Bake for 10 to 12 minutes, or until the fruit is bubbly and the topping is golden brown. Serve warm.

Dark Chocolate Soufflé

Servings: 6
Cooking Time: 15 Minutes
Ingredients:
- 3 eggs, separated
- 1 teaspoon vanilla
- ¼ cup swerve
- 5 tablespoons butter, melted
- 2 tablespoons heavy cream
- 2 tablespoons almond flour
- 2 oz. dark chocolate, melted

Directions:
1. Mix together melted chocolate and butter.
2. In a suitable bowl, whisk egg yolk with sweetener until combined.
3. Add almond flour, heavy cream, and vanilla and whisk well.
4. In a separate bowl, whisk egg white s until soft peaks form.
5. Slowly add the egg white to the chocolate mixture and fold well.
6. Pour chocolate mixture into the ramekins and place into the air fryer.
7. Cook at almost 330 degrees F/ 165 degrees C for 12 minutes.
8. Serve and enjoy.

Blueberry Muffins

Servings: 8
Cooking Time: 14 Minutes
Ingredients:
- ½ cup of sugar alternative
- 1 ⅓ cup of flour
- ⅓ cup of oil
- 2 teaspoons of baking powder
- ¼ teaspoon of salt
- 1 egg
- ½ cup of milk
- 8 muffin cups foil with paper liners or silicone baking cups
- ⅔ cup of frozen and thawed blueberries, or fresh

Directions:
1. Let the air fryer preheat to 330 degrees F/ 165 degrees C.
2. In a suitable bowl, sift together baking powder, sugar, salt, and flour. Mix well
3. In another bowl, add milk, oil, and egg mix it well.
4. To the dry ingredients to the egg mix, mix until combined but do not over mix
5. Add the blueberries carefully. Pour the mixture into muffin paper cups or muffin baking tray
6. Put 4 muffin cups in the air fryer basket.
7. Cook for 12-14 minutes, at 330 degrees F/ 165 degrees C, or until when touch lightly the tops, it should spring back.
8. Cook the remaining muffins accordingly.
9. Serve.

Simple & Tasty Brownies

Servings: 2
Cooking Time: 5 Minutes
Ingredients:
- 2 tablespoons of baking chips
- ⅓ cup of almond flour
- 1 egg
- ½ teaspoon of baking powder
- 3 tablespoons of powdered sweetener sugar alternative
- 2 tablespoons of cocoa powder unsweetened
- 2 tablespoons of chopped pecans
- 4 tablespoons of melted butter

Directions:
1. Let the air fryer preheat to 350 degrees F/ 175 degrees C
2. In a suitable bowl, add cocoa powder, almond flour, Swerve sugar substitute, and baking powder, give it a good mix.
3. Add melted butter and crack in the egg in the dry ingredients.
4. Mix well until combined and smooth.
5. Fold in the chopped pecans and baking chips.
6. Take 2 ramekins to grease them well with softened butter. Add the batter to them.
7. Air fry for 10 minutes. Make sure to place them as far from the heat source from the top in the air fryer.
8. Take the brownies out from the air fryer and let them cool for 5 minutes.
9. Serve with your favorite toppings and enjoy.

Big Chocolate Chip Cookie

Servings: 4
Cooking Time: 9 Minutes
Ingredients:
- Nonstick baking spray with flour
- 3 tablespoons softened butter
- ⅓ cup plus 1 tablespoon brown sugar
- 1 egg yolk
- ½ cup flour
- 2 tablespoons ground white chocolate
- ¼ teaspoon baking soda
- ½ teaspoon vanilla
- ¾ cup chocolate chips

Directions:
1. In medium bowl, beat the butter and brown sugar together until fluffy. Stir in the egg yolk.
2. Add the flour, white chocolate, baking soda, and vanilla, and mix well. Stir in the chocolate chips.
3. Line a 6-by-6-by-2-inch baking pan with parchment paper. Spray the parchment paper with nonstick baking spray with flour.
4. Spread the batter into the prepared pan, leaving a ½-inch border on all sides.
5. Bake for about 9 minutes or until the cookie is light brown and just barely set.
6. Remove the pan from the air fryer and let cool for 10 minutes. Remove the cookie from the pan, remove the parchment paper, and let cool on a wire rack.

Strawberry Cheesecake Rolls

Servings: 12
Cooking Time: 20 Minutes
Ingredients:
- 1 (8-ounce) can crescent rolls
- 4 ounces cream cheese
- 1 tablespoon strawberry preserves
- ⅓ cup sliced fresh strawberries
- Cooking oil

Directions:
1. On a flat work surface, roll out the dough into a large rectangle.
2. Cut the dough into 12 rectangles by making 3 cuts crosswise and 2 cuts lengthwise.
3. Place the cream cheese in a small, microwave-safe bowl. Microwave for 15 seconds to soften.
4. In a medium bowl, combine the cream cheese and strawberry preserves and stir.
5. Scoop 2 teaspoons of the cream cheese and strawberry mixture onto each piece of dough. Spread, but avoid the edges of the dough.
6. Add 2 teaspoons of fresh strawberries to each.
7. Roll up each of the rectangles to create a roll.
8. Spray the air fryer basket with cooking oil.
9. Place the rolls in the basket. Do not stack. Cook in batches. Spray the rolls with cooking oil. Cook for 8 minutes.
10. Allow the rolls to cool for 2 to 3 minutes, then remove from the air fryer.
11. Repeat steps 9 and 10 for the remaining rolls.
12. Cool before serving.

S'mores

Servings: 4 S'mores
Cooking Time: 15 Minutes
Ingredients:
- 4 marshmallows
- 4 graham crackers, divided in half
- 1 milk chocolate, divided

Directions:
1. Put 4 halves of graham crackers into the air fryer basket.
2. Cut off a small piece from the bottom of each marshmallow and put the marshmallow on the crackers, which will help to stick them well.
3. Cook at 375°F for 7–8 minutes until golden-brown.
4. Add on the top the pieces of chocolate and cover with another half of crackers.
5. Continue cooking for about 2 minutes until the chocolate starts melting.
6. Serve and enjoy your S'mores!

Donuts

Servings: 14 Donuts
Cooking Time: 2 Hours
Ingredients:
- 3 cups of all-purpose flour
- 1 cup of milk, warmed to around 110°F
- 4 tablespoons of unsalted melted butter
- 1 large egg
- ¼ cup +1 teaspoon of sugar
- 2 ½ teaspoons of active dry yeast
- ½ teaspoon of kosher salt
- For Glaze:
- 2 cups of powdered sugar
- 6 tablespoons of unsalted melted butter
- 2 teaspoons of vanilla extract
- 2–4 tablespoons of hot water

Directions:
1. Add the warm milk, yeast, and 1 teaspoon of sugar to a large bowl. Stir it for 5–10 minutes until foamy.
2. Add the egg, ¼ cup of sugar, and salt into the milk mixture. Stir it until combined. Pour in the melted butter with 2 cups of flour and mix.
3. Scrape the sides of the bowl down, and add in 1 more cup of flour. Mix it well until the dough starts pulling away from the bowl but leaves sticky. Continue kneading for 5–10 minutes. Cover the bowl with plastic wrap. Leave it for 30 minutes until the dough doubled.
4. Spread some flour on the work surface. Transfer the dough onto it and roll into a ½-¼-inch-thick layer. Cut out donuts with a round cutter (about 3 inches in diameter). Use a smaller cutter (about 1 inch in diameter) and cut out the centers.
5. Transfer the formed donuts onto the oiled parchment paper, and cover them with oiled plastic wrap. Leave it for 20–30 minutes until the dough is doubled.
6. Preheat your air fryer to 350°F. Spray the inside of the basket with some oil.
7. Put the formed donuts in the preheated air fryer in a single layer. Avoid them touching. Lightly spray tops with oil. Cook at 350°F for 4–5 minutes. Repeat this step with the remaining part of donuts and their holes.
8. For making glaze: Meantime, pour the melted butter into a medium bowl. Add in vanilla and powdered sugar. Whisk until combined. Stir in 1 tablespoon of hot water at a time until you reach the desired consistency.
9. After cooling the cooked donuts for a few minutes, glaze them until fully coated. Put donuts on the rack to drip off the excess of the glaze until it hardens.
10. Serve and enjoy your Donuts!

Simple Donuts

Servings: 4
Cooking Time: 15 Minutes
Ingredients:
- 8 ounces' coconut flour 2 tablespoons stevia
- 1 egg, whisked
- 1-½ tablespoons butter, melted
- 4 ounces' coconut milk
- 1 teaspoon baking powder

Directions:
1. Thoroughly mix up all of the ingredients in a bowl.
2. Form donuts from the mixture.
3. Cook the donuts in your air fryer at 370 degrees F/ 185 degrees C for 15 minutes.
4. When cooked, serve and enjoy.

Marble Cheesecake

Servings: 8
Cooking Time: 20 Minutes
Ingredients:
- 1 cup graham cracker crumbs
- 3 tablespoons softened butter
- 1½ (8-ounce) packages cream cheese, softened
- ⅓ cup sugar
- 2 eggs, beaten
- 1 tablespoon flour
- 1 teaspoon vanilla
- ¼ cup chocolate syrup

Directions:
1. For the crust, combine the graham cracker crumbs and butter in a small bowl and mix well. Press into the bottom of a 6-by-6-by-2-inch baking pan and put in the freezer to set.
2. For the filling, combine the cream cheese and sugar in a medium bowl and mix well. Beat in the eggs, one at a time. Add the flour and vanilla.
3. Remove ⅔ cup of the filling to a small bowl and stir in the chocolate syrup until combined.
4. Pour the vanilla filling into the pan with the crust. Drop the chocolate filling over the vanilla filling by the spoonful. With a clean butter knife stir the fillings in a zigzag pattern to marbleize them.
5. Bake for 20 minutes or until the cheesecake is just set.
6. Cool on a wire rack for 1 hour, then chill in the refrigerator until the cheesecake is firm.

Apple Peach Cranberry Crisp

Servings: 8
Cooking Time: 12 Minutes
Ingredients:
- 1 apple, peeled and chopped
- 2 peaches, peeled and chopped
- ⅓ cup dried cranberries
- 2 tablespoons honey
- ⅓ cup brown sugar
- ¼ cup flour
- ½ cup oatmeal
- 3 tablespoons softened butter

Directions:
1. In a 6-by-6-by-2-inch pan, combine the apple, peaches, cranberries, and honey, and mix well.
2. In a medium bowl, combine the brown sugar, flour, oatmeal, and butter, and mix until crumbly. Sprinkle this mixture over the fruit in the pan.
3. Bake for 10 to 12 minutes or until the fruit is bubbly and the topping is golden brown. Serve warm.

Plum Apple Crumble With Cranberries

Servings: 6-7
Cooking Time: 25 Minutes
Ingredients:
- 2 ½ ounces caster sugar
- ⅓ cup oats
- ⅔ cup flour
- ½ stick butter, chilled
- 1 tablespoon cold water
- 1 tablespoon honey
- ½ teaspoon ground mace
- ¼ pound plums, pitted and chopped
- ¼ pound apples, cored and chopped
- 1 tablespoon lemon juice
- ½ teaspoon vanilla paste
- 1 cup cranberries

Directions:
1. On a flat kitchen surface, plug your air fryer and turn it on.
2. Gently coat your cake pan with cooking oil or spray.
3. Before cooking, heat your air fryer to 390 degrees F/ 200 degrees C for about 4 to 5 minutes.
4. Mix the lemon juice, sugar, honey, mace, apples, and plums in a medium sized bowl.
5. Place the fruits onto the cake pan.
6. In a second medium sized bowl, mix thoroughly the rest of the ingredients and add the fruit mixture on the top. Transfer to the cake pan.
7. Bake the apple crumble in the preheated air fryer for 20 minutes.
8. When cooked, remove from the air fryer and serve warm.

Coconut Walnuts

Servings: 12
Cooking Time: 40 Minutes
Ingredients:
- 1 and ¼ cups almond flour
- 1 cup swerve
- 1 cup butter, melted
- ½ cup coconut cream
- 1 and ½ cups coconut, flaked
- 1 egg yolk
- ¾ cup walnuts, chopped
- ½ teaspoon vanilla extract

Directions:
1. Stir the flour, half of the swerve and half of the butter well, then press the mixture on the cooking pan of your air fryer.
2. Cook the mixture at 350 degrees F/ 175 degrees C for 15 minutes.
3. While cooking the mixture, heat the rest of the ingredients in a pan for 1 to 2 minutes.
4. Arrange the heated mixture to the air fryer and continue to cook for 25 minutes more.
5. Before serving, cool the food down and cut into bars.

Cinnamon Sugar Donut Holes

Servings:16
Cooking Time: 20 Minutes
Ingredients:
- 1 (8-ounce) can jumbo biscuit dough
- Cooking oil
- 1 tablespoon stevia
- 2 tablespoons cinnamon

Directions:
1. Form the biscuit dough evenly into 16 balls, 1 to 1½ inches thick.
2. Spray the air fryer basket with cooking oil.
3. Place 8 donut holes in the air fryer. Do not stack. Spray them with cooking oil. Cook for 4 minutes.
4. Open the air fryer and flip the donut holes. Cook for an additional 4 minutes.
5. Remove the cooked donut holes, then repeat steps 3 and 4 for the remaining 8 donut holes. Allow the donut holes to cool.
6. In a small bowl, combine the stevia and cinnamon and stir.
7. Spritz the donut holes with cooking oil. Dip the donut holes in the cinnamon and sugar mixture, and serve.

Banana Chocolate Muffins

Servings: 8
Cooking Time: 30 Minutes
Ingredients:
- Wet Mix
- 3 tablespoons of milk
- 1 teaspoon of Nutella
- 4 Cavendish size, ripe bananas
- ½ cup sugar
- 1 teaspoon of vanilla essence
- 2 large eggs
- Dry Mix
- 1 teaspoon of baking powder
- 1 ¼ cup of whole wheat flour
- 1 teaspoon of baking soda
- 1 teaspoon of cinnamon
- 2 tablespoons of cocoa powder
- 1 teaspoon of salt
- Optional
- 1 handful chopped walnuts
- Fruits, Dried slices
- Chocolate sprinkles

Directions:
1. With the fork, in a suitable bowl, mash up the bananas, add all the wet ingredients to it, and mix well.
2. Sift all the dry ingredients so they combine well. Add into the wet ingredients. Carefully fold both ingredients together. Do not over mix.
3. Then add in the diced walnuts, slices of dried up fruits, and chocolate sprinkles.
4. Let the air fryer preheat to 250 degrees F/ 120 degrees C.
5. Add the batter into muffin cups before that, spray them with oil generously.
6. Air fryer them for at least ½ an hour, or until a toothpick comes out clean.
7. Serve.

Curry Peaches, Pears, And Plums

Servings: 8
Cooking Time: 5 Minutes
Ingredients:
- 2 peaches
- 2 firm pears
- 2 plums
- 2 tablespoons melted butter
- 1 tablespoon honey
- 2 to 3 teaspoons curry powder

Directions:
1. Preheat the air fryer to 325°F (163°C).
2. Cut the peaches in half, remove the pits, and cut each half in half again. Cut the pears in half, core them, and remove the stem. Cut each half in half again. Do the same with the plums.
3. Spread a large sheet of heavy-duty foil on the work surface. Arrange the fruit on the foil and drizzle with the butter and honey. Sprinkle with the curry powder.
4. Wrap the fruit in the foil, making sure to leave some air space in the packet.
5. Put the foil package in the basket and bake for 5 to 8 minutes, shaking the basket once during the cooking time, until the fruit is soft.
6. Serve immediately.

Berry Crumble

Servings: 4
Cooking Time: 15 Minutes
Ingredients:
- For the Filling:
- 2 cups mixed berries
- 2 tablespoons sugar
- 1 tablespoon cornstarch
- 1 tablespoon fresh lemon juice
- For the Topping:
- ¼ cup all-purpose flour
- ¼ cup rolled oats
- 1 tablespoon sugar
- 2 tablespoons cold unsalted butter, cut into small cubes
- Whipped cream or ice cream (optional)

Directions:
1. Preheat the air fryer to 400°F (204°C).
2. For the filling: In a round baking pan, gently mix the berries, sugar, cornstarch, and lemon juice until thoroughly combined.
3. For the topping: In a small bowl, combine the flour, oats, and sugar. Stir the butter into the flour mixture until the mixture has the consistency of bread crumbs.
4. Sprinkle the topping over the berries.
5. Put the pan in the air fryer basket and air fry for 15 minutes. Let cool for 5 minutes on a wire rack.
6. Serve topped with whipped cream or ice cream, if desired.

Almond Cherry Bars

Servings: 12
Cooking Time: 35 Minutes
Ingredients:
- 2 eggs, lightly beaten
- 1 cup erythritol
- ½ tsp vanilla
- ¼ cup water
- ½ cup butter, softened
- ¾ cup cherries, pitted
- 1 ½ cup almond flour
- 1 tablespoon xanthan gum
- ½ teaspoon salt

Directions:
1. Mix vanilla, butter, salt, almond flour, the beaten eggs, and erythritol together in a bowl to form a dough.
2. Transfer the dough to a baking dish that fits in your air fryer and press the dough to flatten the surface.
3. Bake in your air fryer at 375 degrees F/ 190 degrees C for 10 minutes.
4. While baking, stir together the xanthan gum, water, and cherries in a separate bowl.
5. When the cooking time is up, add the cherry mixture over the dough. Cook again for 25 minutes.
6. Once cooked, cut the dough into your desired size and serve.

Coconut Cupcakes With Cardamom

Servings: 4
Cooking Time: 5 Minutes
Ingredients:
- ½ cup coconut flour
- ⅓ cup coconut milk
- 2 eggs
- 1 tablespoon coconut oil, melted
- 1 teaspoon vanilla
- A pinch of ground cardamom
- ½ cup coconut chips

Directions:
1. Mix the flour, coconut milk, eggs, coconut oil, vanilla, and cardamom in a suitable bowl.
2. Let it stand for 20 minutes. Spoon this prepared batter into a greased muffin tin.
3. Cook at almost 230 degrees F/ 110 degrees C for 4 to 5 minutes or until golden brown. Repeat with the remaining batter.
4. Decorate your cupcakes with coconut chips.
5. Serve

Moist Cinnamon Muffins

Servings: 20
Cooking Time: 12 Minutes
Ingredients:
- 1 tablespoon cinnamon
- 1 teaspoon baking powder
- 2 scoops vanilla protein: powder
- ½ cup almond flour
- ½ cup coconut oil
- ½ cup pumpkin puree
- ½ cup almond butter

Directions:
1. Before cooking, heat your air fryer to 325 degrees F/ 160 degrees C.
2. Combine together cinnamon, baking powder, vanilla protein: powder, and almond flour in a large bowl.
3. Then mix the dry mixture together with the coconut oil, pumpkin puree, and almond butter until well incorporated.
4. Divide the batter into the silicone muffin molds.
5. Cook in batches in your air fryer for 12 minutes.
6. Serve and enjoy!

Chocolate Donuts

Servings: 8
Cooking Time: 20 Minutes
Ingredients:
- 1 (8-ounce) can jumbo biscuits
- Cooking oil
- Chocolate sauce, such as Hershey's

Directions:
1. Separate the biscuit dough into 8 biscuits and place them on a flat work surface. Use a small circle cookie cutter or a biscuit cutter to cut a hole in the center of each biscuit. You can also cut the holes using a knife.
2. Spray the air fryer basket with cooking oil.
3. Place 4 donuts in the air fryer. Do not stack. Spray with cooking oil. Cook for 4 minutes.
4. Open the air fryer and flip the donuts. Cook for an additional 4 minutes.
5. Remove the cooked donuts from the air fryer, then repeat steps 3 and 4 for the remaining 4 donuts.
6. Drizzle chocolate sauce over the donuts and enjoy while warm. (For homemade chocolate sauce, see Ingredient tip in Fried Bananas with Chocolate Sauce, here.)

Vanilla Cobbler With Hazelnut

Servings: 4
Cooking Time: 30 Minutes
Ingredients:
- ¼ cup heavy cream
- 1 egg, beaten
- ½ cup almond flour
- 1 teaspoon vanilla extract
- 2 tablespoons butter, softened
- ¼ cup hazelnuts, chopped

Directions:
1. Mix up heavy cream, egg, almond flour, vanilla extract, and butter.
2. Then whisk the mixture gently. At 325 degrees F/ 160 degrees C, preheat your air fryer.
3. Layer its air fryer basket with baking paper.
4. Pour ½ part of the batter in the baking pan, flatten it gently and top with hazelnuts.
5. Then pour the remaining batter over the hazelnuts and place the pan in the air fryer.
6. Cook the cobbler for 30 minutes.

Chickpea Brownies

Servings: 6
Cooking Time: 20 Minutes
Ingredients:
- Vegetable oil
- 1 (15-ounce / 425-g) can chickpeas, drained and rinsed
- 4 large eggs
- ⅓ cup coconut oil, melted
- ⅓ cup honey
- 3 tablespoons unsweetened cocoa powder
- 1 tablespoon espresso powder (optional)
- 1 teaspoon baking powder
- 1 teaspoon baking soda
- ½ cup chocolate chips

Directions:
1. Preheat the air fryer to 325°F (163°C).
2. Generously grease a baking pan with vegetable oil.
3. In a blender or food processor, combine the chickpeas, eggs, coconut oil, honey, cocoa powder, espresso powder (if using), baking powder, and baking soda. Blend or process until smooth. Transfer to the prepared pan and stir in the chocolate chips by hand.
4. Set the pan in the air fryer basket and bake for 20 minutes, or until a toothpick inserted into the center comes out clean.
5. Let cool in the pan on a wire rack for 30 minutes before cutting into squares.
6. Serve immediately.

Cocoa Nutmeg Cake

Servings: 8
Cooking Time: 40 Minutes
Ingredients:
- ½ cup heavy cream
- 3 eggs, beaten
- 3 tablespoons cocoa powder
- 1 teaspoon vanilla extract
- 1 teaspoon baking powder
- 3 tablespoons Erythritol
- 1 cup almond flour
- ¼ teaspoon ground nutmeg
- 1 tablespoon avocado oil
- 1 teaspoon Splenda

Directions:
1. In a bowl, stir the heavy cream, eggs and cocoa powder well until smooth, then add vanilla extract, baking powder, Erythritol, almond flour, ground nutmeg, avocado oil and whisk well.
2. Pour the mixture in the cake mold.
3. Use the toothpick to pierce the foil.
4. Arrange the cake mold to the cooking basket and cook in the air fryer at 360 degrees F/ 180 degrees C for 40 minutes.
5. When cooked, sprinkle the Splenda on the top after cooling completely.
6. Serve and enjoy.

Erythritol Vanilla Butter Pie

Servings: 8
Cooking Time: 20 Minutes
Ingredients:
- 1 egg
- 2 tablespoons erythritol
- ½ cup butter, melted
- 1 teaspoon vanilla
- 1 cup almond flour
- 1 teaspoon baking soda
- 1 tablespoon vinegar

Directions:
1. Mix almond flour and baking soda in a suitable bowl.
2. In a separate bowl, whisk the egg with sweetener and vanilla.
3. Pour whisk egg, vinegar, and butter in almond flour and mix until dough is formed.
4. At 340 degrees F/ 170 degrees C, preheat your air fryer.
5. Roll dough using the rolling pin in air fryer basket size.
6. Place rolled dough in air fryer basket and cook for 20 minutes.
7. Slice and serve.

Chocolate S'mores

Servings: 12
Cooking Time: 3 Minutes
Ingredients:
- 12 whole cinnamon graham crackers
- 2 (1.55-ounce / 44-g) chocolate bars, broken into 12 pieces
- 12 marshmallows

Directions:
1. Preheat the air fryer to 350°F (177°C).
2. Halve each graham cracker into 2 squares.
3. Put 6 graham cracker squares in the air fryer. Do not stack. Put a piece of chocolate into each. Bake for 2 minutes.
4. Open the air fryer and add a marshmallow onto each piece of melted chocolate. Bake for 1 additional minute.
5. Remove the cooked s'mores from the air fryer, then repeat steps 2 and 3 for the remaining 6 s'mores.
6. Top with the remaining graham cracker squares and serve.

Jelly Doughnuts

Servings: 8
Cooking Time: 5 Minutes
Ingredients:
- 1 (16.3-ounce / 462-g) package large refrigerator biscuits
- Cooking spray
- 1¼ cups good-quality raspberry jam
- Confectioners' sugar, for dusting

Directions:
1. Preheat the air fryer to 350°F (177°C).
2. Separate biscuits into 8 rounds. Spray both sides of rounds lightly with oil.
3. Spray the basket with oil and place 3 to 4 rounds in the basket. Air fry for 5 minutes, or until golden brown. Transfer to a wire rack; let cool. Repeat with the remaining rounds.
4. Fill a pastry bag, fitted with small plain tip, with raspberry jam; use tip to poke a small hole in the side of each doughnut, then fill the centers with the jam. Dust doughnuts with confectioners' sugar.
5. Serve immediately.

Simple Pineapple Sticks

Servings: 4
Cooking Time: 10 Minutes
Ingredients:
- ½ fresh pineapple, cut into sticks
- ¼ cup desiccated coconut

Directions:
1. Preheat the air fryer to 400°F (204°C).
2. Coat the pineapple sticks in the desiccated coconut and put each one in the air fryer basket.
3. Air fry for 10 minutes.
4. Serve immediately

Vanilla Chocolate Bites

Servings: 8
Cooking Time: 13 Minutes
Ingredients:
- 2 cups plain flour
- 2 tablespoons cocoa powder
- ½ cup icing sugar
- Pinch of ground cinnamon
- 1 teaspoon vanilla extract
- ¾ cup chilled butter
- ¼ cup chocolate, chopped into eight chunks

Directions:
1. In a suitable bowl, mix the flour, icing sugar, cocoa powder, cinnamon, and vanilla extract.
2. Cut the butter and mix to make a smooth dough.
3. Then divide the dough into 8 equal-sized balls.
4. Insert 1 chocolate chunk in the center of each dough ball and cover with the dough thoroughly.
5. Place the dough balls into the baking pan.
6. Set the cook time to 8 minutes. Set the temperature at 355 degrees F/ 180 degrees C.
7. Arrange this pan in air fry basket and insert it in the air fryer.
8. After 8 minutes of cook, set the temperature at 320 degrees F/ 160 degrees C for 5 minutes.
9. Place the hot baking pan onto the wire rack to cool before serving.

Cheese Muffins With Cinnamon

Servings: 10
Cooking Time: 16 Minutes
Ingredients:
- 2 eggs
- ½ cup erythritol
- 8 ounces cream cheese
- 1 teaspoon ground cinnamon
- ½ tsp vanilla

Directions:
1. Before cooking, heat your air fryer to 325 degrees F/ 160 degrees C.
2. Mix together vanilla, erythritol, eggs, and cream cheese until smooth.
3. Divide the batter into the silicone muffin molds. Top the muffins with cinnamon.
4. In the air fryer basket, transfer the muffin molds.
5. Cook in your air fryer for 16 minutes.
6. Serve and enjoy!

Fudgy Chocolate Brownies

Servings: 6
Cooking Time: 16 Minutes
Ingredients:
- 3 eggs
- ½ teaspoon baking powder
- ¾ cup erythritol
- 2 oz. dark chocolate
- ¾ cup butter softened
- ½ cup almond flour
- ¼ cup of cocoa powder

Directions:
1. At 325 degrees F/ 160 degrees C, preheat your air fryer.
2. Grease its air fryer basket with cooking spray and set aside.
3. In a suitable bowl, mix together chocolate and butter and microwave for 30 seconds or until melted. Stir well.
4. Mix together almond flour, baking powder, cocoa powder, and sweetener.
5. In a suitable bowl, beat eggs using a hand mixer. Add chocolate-butter mixture and beat until combined.
6. Slowly stir in dry recipe ingredients and mix until well combined.
7. Pour batter into the prepared dish and place into the air fryer.
8. Cook for 16 minutes.
9. Slice and serve.

Honey-roasted Pears With Ricotta

Servings: 4
Cooking Time:18 To 23 Minutes
Ingredients:
- 2 large Bosc pears, halved and seeded (see Tip)
- 3 tablespoons honey
- 1 tablespoon unsalted butter
- ½ teaspoon ground cinnamon
- ¼ cup walnuts, chopped
- ¼ cup part skim low-fat ricotta cheese, divided

Directions:
1. In a 6-by-2-inch pan, place the pears cut-side up.
2. In a small microwave-safe bowl, melt the honey, butter, and cinnamon. Brush this mixture over the cut sides of the pears.
3. Pour 3 tablespoons of water around the pears in the pan. Roast the pears for 18 to 23 minutes, or until tender when pierced with a fork and slightly crisp on the edges, basting once with the liquid in the pan.
4. Carefully remove the pears from the pan and place on a serving plate. Drizzle each with some liquid from the pan, sprinkle the walnuts on top, and serve with a spoonful of ricotta cheese.

Cardamom And Vanilla Custard

Servings:2
Cooking Time: 25 Minutes
Ingredients:
- 1 cup whole milk
- 1 large egg
- 2 tablespoons plus 1 teaspoon sugar
- ¼ teaspoon vanilla bean paste or pure vanilla extract
- ¼ teaspoon ground cardamom, plus more for sprinkling

Directions:
1. Preheat the air fryer to 350°F (177°C).
2. In a medium bowl, beat together the milk, egg, sugar, vanilla, and cardamom.
3. Put two ramekins in the air fryer basket. Divide the mixture between the ramekins. Sprinkle lightly with cardamom. Cover each ramekin tightly with aluminum foil. Bake for 25 minutes, or until a toothpick inserted in the center comes out clean.
4. Let the custards cool on a wire rack for 5 to 10 minutes.
5. Serve warm, or refrigerate until cold and serve chilled.

Lemon Butter Bars

Servings: 8
Cooking Time: 35 Minutes
Ingredients:
- ½ cup butter, melted
- 1 cup Erythritol
- 1 and ¾ cups almond flour
- 3 eggs, whisked
- Zest of 1 lemon, grated Juice of 3 lemons

Directions:
1. In a bowl, stir 1 cup flour, half of the Erythritol and butter well, then press the mixture into the cooking pan lined with parchment paper.
2. Cook the mixture at 350 degrees F/ 175 degrees C for 10 minutes.
3. While cooking, prepare a bowl, whisk the rest of flour, the remaining Erythritol and other ingredients well.
4. When the mixture cooked, spread the mixture over the it and cook at 350 degrees F/ 175 degrees C for 25 minutes more.
5. Cool down and cut into bars before enjoying.

Stuffed Apples

Servings: 4
Cooking Time:12 To 17 Minutes
Ingredients:
- 4 medium apples, rinsed and patted dry (see Tip)
- 2 tablespoons freshly squeezed lemon juice
- ¼ cup golden raisins
- 3 tablespoons chopped walnuts
- 3 tablespoons dried cranberries
- 2 tablespoons packed brown sugar
- ⅓ cup apple cider

Directions:
1. Cut a strip of peel from the top of each apple and remove the core, being careful not to cut through the bottom of the apple. Sprinkle the cut parts of the apples with lemon juice and place in a 6-by-2-inch pan.
2. In a small bowl, stir together the raisins, walnuts, cranberries, and brown sugar. Stuff one-fourth of this mixture into each apple.
3. Pour the apple cider around the apples in the pan.
4. Bake in the air fryer for 12 to 17 minutes, or until the apples are tender when pierced with a fork. Serve immediately.

Chocolate Oatmeal Cookies

Servings: 8
Cooking Time: 8 Minutes
Ingredients:
- ⅓ cup of tahini
- ¼ cup of walnuts
- ¼ cup of maple syrup
- ¼ cup of chocolate chunks
- ¼ teaspoon of salt
- 2 tablespoons of almond flour
- 1 teaspoon of vanilla
- 1 cup of gluten-free oat flakes
- 1 teaspoon of cinnamon

Directions:
1. At 350 degrees F/ 175 degrees C, preheat your air fryer.
2. In a big bowl, add cinnamon, the maple syrup, the tahini, salt, and vanilla.
3. Mix well, then add in the walnuts, oat flakes, and almond meal.
4. Then fold in the chocolate chips gently.
5. Now the mix is ready, take a full tablespoon of mixture, separate into 8 amounts.
6. Wet damp hands, press them on a baking tray or with a spatula.
7. Place 4 cookies, or more depending on your air fryer size, line the air fryer basket with parchment paper in 1 single layer.
8. Let them cook for 5-6 minutes at 350 degrees F/ 175 degrees C, air fry for more minutes if you like them crispy.
9. Serve.

Vanilla Cookies

Servings: 12
Cooking Time: 15 Minutes
Ingredients:
- 2 cups almond flour 1 cup swerve
- ¼ cup butter, melted 1 egg
- 2 teaspoons ginger, grated
- ¼ teaspoon nutmeg, ground
- ¼ teaspoon cinnamon powder
- 1 teaspoon vanilla extract

Directions:
1. Thoroughly mix up all of the ingredients in a bowl.
2. Form small balls from the mixture with a spoon, then arrange them to the cooking pan lined with parchment patter and flatten them.
3. Cook the balls in your air fryer at 360 degrees F/ 180 degrees C for 15 minutes.
4. Before serving, cool them.

Buttery Shortbread Sticks

Servings: 10
Cooking Time: 22 Minutes
Ingredients:
- ⅓ cup caster sugar
- 1 2/3 cups plain flour
- ¾ cup butter

Directions:
1. In a suitable bowl, mix the sugar and flour.
2. Add the butter and stir until it makes a smooth dough.
3. Cut the dough into ten equal-sized sticks. With a fork, lightly prick the sticks.
4. Place the sticks into the lightly greased baking pan.
5. Set the cook time to 12 minutes.
6. At 355 degrees F/ 180 degrees C, preheat your air fryer.
7. Arrange the pan in preheat air fry basket and insert it in the air fryer.
8. Place the baking pan to cool for about 5-10 minutes.
9. Serve.

Vanilla Muffins With Pecans

Servings: 12
Cooking Time: 15 Minutes
Ingredients:
- 4 eggs
- 1 teaspoon vanilla
- ¼ cup almond milk
- 2 tablespoons butter, melted
- ½ cup swerve
- 1 teaspoon psyllium husk
- 1 tablespoon baking powder
- ½ cup pecans, chopped
- ½ teaspoon ground cinnamon
- 2 teaspoons allspice
- 1 ½ cups almond flour

Directions:
1. At 370 degrees F/ 185 degrees C, preheat your air fryer.
2. Beat eggs, almond milk, vanilla, sweetener, and butter in a suitable bowl using a hand mixer until smooth.
3. Add remaining recipe ingredients and mix until well combined.
4. Pour batter into the silicone muffin molds and place into the air fryer basket in batches.
5. Cook muffins for almost 15 minutes.
6. Serve and enjoy.

Creamy Cheesecake Bites

Servings: 16
Cooking Time: 2 Minutes
Ingredients:
- 8 ounces cream cheese, softened
- 2 tablespoons erythritol
- ½ cup almond flour
- ½ tsp vanilla
- 4 tablespoons heavy cream
- ½ cup erythritol

Directions:
1. In a stand mixer, mix cream cheese, 2 tbsp. heavy cream, vanilla, and ½ cup erythritol until smooth.
2. Line a plate with parchment paper and spread the cream cheese onto the parchment.
3. Refrigerate for 1 hour.
4. Mix together 2 tbsp. Erythritol and almond flour in a small bowl.
5. Drip the remaining heavy cream over the cheesecake bites and dip in the almond flour mixture to coat.
6. Arrange evenly the cheesecake bites inside the air fryer basket and cook in the air fryer at 350 degrees F/ 175 degrees C for 2 minutes.
7. Halfway cooking, check the cheesecake bites to ensure they are still frozen.
8. Serve with chocolate syrup on the top.

Apple, Peach, And Cranberry Crisp

Servings: 8
Cooking Time: 12 Minutes
Ingredients:
- 1 apple, peeled and chopped
- 2 peaches, peeled and chopped
- ⅓ cup dried cranberries
- 2 tablespoons honey
- ⅓ cup brown sugar
- ¼ cup flour
- ½ cup oatmeal
- 3 tablespoons softened butter

Directions:
1. Preheat the air fryer to 370°F (188°C).
2. In a baking pan, combine the apple, peaches, cranberries, and honey, and mix well.
3. In a medium bowl, combine the brown sugar, flour, oatmeal, and butter, and mix until crumbly. Sprinkle this mixture over the fruit in the pan.
4. Bake for 10 to 12 minutes or until the fruit is bubbly and the topping is golden brown. Serve warm.

Pear And Apple Crisp

Servings: 6
Cooking Time: 20 Minutes
Ingredients:
- ½ pound (227 g) apples, cored and chopped
- ½ pound (227 g) pears, cored and chopped
- 1 cup flour
- 1 cup sugar
- 1 tablespoon butter
- 1 teaspoon ground cinnamon
- ¼ teaspoon ground cloves
- 1 teaspoon vanilla extract
- ¼ cup chopped walnuts
- Whipped cream, for serving

Directions:
1. Preheat the air fryer to 340°F (171°C).
2. Lightly grease a baking dish and place the apples and pears inside.
3. Combine the rest of the ingredients, minus the walnuts and the whipped cream, until a coarse, crumbly texture is achieved.
4. Pour the mixture over the fruits and spread it evenly. Top with the chopped walnuts.
5. Bake for 20 minutes or until the top turns golden brown.
6. Serve at room temperature with whipped cream.

Baklava Purses

Servings: 4 Servings
Cooking Time: 25 Minutes
Ingredients:
- 4 stacks of 8 sheets of phyllo dough (4x4 inches)
- 1 egg
- ¼ cup of chopped walnuts
- 1 tablespoon of chopped pistachios
- 2 tablespoons of melted butter
- 1 teaspoon of honey
- Cinnamon, to taste
- Orange zest, to taste

Directions:
1. Preheat your air fryer to 375°F. Grease the inside of the air fryer basket with some oil.
2. Grease every second sheet of the phyllo dough with the melted butter. Place the chopped walnuts in the center, then pour the honey on them, and sprinkle some orange zest and cinnamon.
3. Press the corners together and push down into the honey to stick them and made it look like a "purse."
4. Put the prepared baklava in the preheated air fryer. Cook at 375°F for 6–8 minutes until golden-brown crispy. Top with the chopped pistachios.
5. Repeat the last 2 steps until all dough is used.
6. Serve with honey and enjoy your Baklava Purses!

RECIPES INDEX

A

Air Fried Beef Ribs 71

Air Fried Brussels Sprout 41

Air Fried Potatoes With Olives 49

Air Fryer Naked Chicken Tenders 54

Air-fried Chicken Wings And Waffles 22

Alfredo Chicken With Mushrooms 62

Almond Cherry Bars 96

Apple Peach Cranberry Crisp 94

Apple, Peach, And Cranberry Crisp 102

Apple-peach Crisp 91

Apricot-glazed Turkey Tenderloin 61

Artichoke-spinach Dip 36

Asian Sirloin Steaks With Worcestershire Sauce 73

Asian Swordfish 87

Avocado And Egg Burrito 18

Awesome Parmesan Shrimp 78

B

Bacon And Broccoli Bread Pudding 21

Bacon And Cabbage 40

Bacon Tater Tots 27

Bacon-wrapped Chicken 51

Baked Eggs 13

Baked Eggs With Mascarpone 23

Baked Parmesan Eggs With Kielbasa 26

Baked Ricotta 31

Baklava Purses 103

Banana Bread 24

Banana Chocolate Muffins 95

Banana-nut French Toast 18

Banana-pecan French Toast 20

Barbecued Chicken 56

Basmati Risotto 45

Beef Chuck With Brussels Sprouts 72

Beef Taco Chimichangas 67

Beer Squid 83

Berry Crumble 96

Best Damn Pork Chops 67

Big Chocolate Chip Cookie 92

Black Bean And Tomato Chili 48

Blackened Chicken Breasts 61

Blueberry Muffins 91

Breakfast Cobbler With Blueberries 15

Breakfast Granola With Cinnamon 21

Broccoli Cheese Tots 50

Broccoli With Paprika 47

Bruschetta-stuffed Chicken 60

Buffalo Chicken Bites 29

Buffalo Chicken Taquitos 54

Burgundy Beef Dish With Egg Noodles 66

Buttered Kale Mix 46

Buttermilk Country-fried Chicken Wings 54

Buttery Shortbread Sticks 102

C

Cajun Fish Cakes 86

Cajun Lemon Branzino 79

Cajun Salmon Burgers 82

Cajun Seasoned Bratwurst With Vegetables 70

Cajun Shrimp With Veggie 86

Cajun Zucchini Chips 29

Canadian Bacon And Cheese English Muffins 17

Cardamom And Vanilla Custard 100

Cashew Stuffed Mushrooms 42
Cauliflower Wings With Buffalo Sauce 34
Cheddar Frittata 25
Cheddar Mushroom Taquitos 23
Cheddar Peppers 18
Cheese And Mushroom Taquitos 13
Cheese Broccoli With Basil 44
Cheese Ground Pork 75
Cheese Muffins With Cinnamon 100
Cheese Spinach 42
Chermoula Beet Roast 40
Chicken And Carrot 63
Chicken And Onion Sausages 62
Chicken Fillets With Lemon Pepper & Cheddar Cheese 63
Chickpea Brownies 98
Chocolate Donuts 97
Chocolate Oatmeal Cookies 101
Chocolate S'mores 99
Cilantro-lime Fried Shrimp 88
Cinnamon And Sugar Peaches 34
Cinnamon Apple Chips 28
Cinnamon Sugar Donut Holes 95
Classical Buffalo Wings 57
Classical French Frittata 14
Classical Greek Keftedes 55
Cocoa Nutmeg Cake 98
Coconut Cupcakes With Cardamom 97
Coconut Muffins With Jalapeno 13
Coconut Shrimp 85
Coconut Veggie And Eggs Bake 20
Coconut Walnuts 95
Coconut-crusted Shrimp 29
Crab Cakes 85

Cranberry Turkey Quesadillas 57
Creamy Broccoli Omelet 16
Creamy Cauliflower Mash 49
Creamy Cheesecake Bites 102
Creamy Savory Salmon 84
Creamy Soufflés 22
Creamy Tuna With Zucchinis 81
Creole Pork Chops 66
Crispy Black Pepperoni Chips 38
Crispy Brussels Sprouts 45
Crispy Chicken Nuggets With Turnip 57
Crispy Chicken Wings 61
Crispy Chickpeas 44
Crispy Phyllo Artichoke Triangles 34
Crispy Vegetable Nuggets 30
Crumbs Crusted Shrimp 88
Crunchy Chicken And Ranch Wraps 56
Crunchy Zucchini Fries With Parmesan 27
Cube Steak 69
Curry Peaches, Pears, And Plums 96

D
Dark Chocolate Soufflé 91
Delectable Fish Nuggets 37
Delectable Pork Chops 74
Delicious Grouper Filets 79
Delicious Zucchini Crackers 28
Dijon Chicken Breasts 50
Dill Chicken Strips 58
Donuts 93

E
Easy Air Fried Salmon 80
Erythritol Vanilla Butter Pie 98

F
Fajita Stuffed Chicken Roll-ups 55
Fish And Vegetable Tacos 80

Fish Mania With Mustard 89

Flavor Calamari With Mediterranean Sauce 81

Flavored Salmon Grill With Oregano & Cumin 90

Flavorful Kale Chips 30

Flounder Filets With Parmesan Cheese 84

Fried Brussel Sprouts 44

Fried Buffalo Chicken Taquitos 58

Frittata 17

Fudgy Chocolate Brownies 100

G

Garlic And Sesame Carrots 46

Garlic Cauliflower Appetizer 28

Garlic Scallops With Parsley 81

Garlic Sesame Broccoli 27

Garlic Shrimp 88

Garlic Soy Chicken Thighs 53

Garlic Spinach Dip 26

Garlicky Vegetable Rainbow Fritters 40

Ginger Salmon Fillet 80

Glazed Beef With Fruits 69

Glazed Fillets 86

Glazed Salmon With Soy Sauce 84

Gorgonzola Mushrooms With Horseradish Mayo 47

Grilled Chicken With Salsa Verde 64

Grilled Tomatoes With Herbs 30

Ground Sausage Casserole 20

H

Hash Brown Bruschetta 32

Healthy Cardamom Salmon 82

Healthy Salmon With Cardamom 87

Healthy Vegetable Patties 56

Hearty Blueberry Oatmeal 16

Hearty Cheddar Biscuits 17

Herbed Chicken And Broccoli 60

Herbed Potatoes With Tomato Sauce 48

Herbed Radishes 49

Herbed Vegetable Mélange 41

Herb-roasted Vegetables 41

Herbs Chicken Drumsticks With Tamari Sauce 59

Honey-roasted Pears With Ricotta 100

Hot Egg Cups 14

I

Italian Chicken And Veggies 59

Italian-style Cheeseburgers With Cheese Slices 71

J

Jalapeño Cheese Balls 32

Jelly Doughnuts 99

K

Kale And Brussels Sprouts 40

Kidney Beans Oatmeal In Peppers 46

L

Lamb Burger 65

Lamb Meatballs 68

Lemon Butter Bars 101

Lemon Chicken In Oyster Sauce 58

Lemon Fennel With Sunflower Seeds 49

Lemon Salmon With Chili 90

Lemony Chicken Drumsticks 38

Lime Trout With Parsley 87

Lush Vegetables Roast 39

M

Marble Cheesecake 94

Mascarpone Mushrooms 45

Mashed Chives And Celery 47

Meatballs In Spicy Tomato Sauce 65

Mexican Beef Muffins With Tomato Sauce 35

Mexican Potato Skins 31

Mexican Sheet Pan Dinner 64

Mini Shrimp Frittata 19

Mint Lemon Squash 43

Mixed Berry Muffins 24
Moist Cinnamon Muffins 97
Montreal Steak 73
Mozzarella Arancini 38
Mozzarella Beef Brisket 68
Mozzarella Veggie Tacos 48
Mushroom And Asparagus Frittata 16
Mustard-crusted Fish Fillets 82

O
Olive Oil Sweet Potato Chips 37
Olives And Eggs Medley 21
Orange Chicken 51
Orange Pork Tenderloin 76
Oregano Pollock With Capers 89

P
Pancetta-wrapped Scallops With Pancetta Slices 80
Parsley Saltine Fillets 86
Pear And Apple Crisp 103
Pesto Fish Finger Sandwich 83
Pigs In A Blanket 28
Pita And Pepperoni Pizza 23
Plum Apple Crumble With Cranberries 94
Pork Cutlets 77
Pork Tenderloin With Bell Pepper 66
Portobello Pizzas 44
Potato And Prosciutto Salad 74
Potato Pastries 33
Potato With Creamy Cheese 43
Potato-nut Casserole Dish 39
Provolone Zucchini Balls 39
Pumpkin Donut Holes 14

Q
Quick Paella 87

R
Ranch Broccoli With Cheddar 31
Ritzy Skirt Steak Fajitas 77
Roast Beef And Brown Rice 72
Roasted Bell Peppers With Garlic 50
Roasted Brussels Sprouts 47
Roasted Spiced Broccoli With Masala 48
Rosemary Baked Cashews 35
Rosemary Ribeye Steaks 70
Rotisserie Whole Chicken 60

S
S'mores 93
Salmon Patties 85
Salmon Patty Bites 83
Sausage And Cream Cheese Biscuits 15
Sausage, Peppers, And Onions 75
Savory Roasted Sweet Potatoes 46
Scalloped Mixed Vegetables 43
Scotch Eggs 22
Scramble Casserole With Cheddar 25
Scrambled Eggs With Spinach 24
Seasoned Chicken Breast 59
Sesame Chicken Tenders 62
Shrimp And Rice Frittata 19
Simple & Tasty Brownies 92
Simple & Tasty Pork Sandwiches 78
Simple Curried Sweet Potato Fries 30
Simple Donuts 93
Simple Eggplant Spread 15
Simple Pineapple Sticks 99
Simple Pork Chops 76
Simple Rib-eye Steak 71
Sizzling Beef Fajitas 70
Southwest Stuffed Mushrooms 32
Spiced Cauliflower Rice With Zucchini 25
Spiced Lamb Kebabs 67

Spiced Pork Chops 66

Spicy And Crispy Duck 63

Spicy Asian Chicken Thighs With Soy Sauce 61

Spicy Cauliflower Roast 42

Spicy Chickpeas 35

Spicy Cocktail Wieners 38

Spicy Coconut Chicken Wings 52

Spicy Jumbo Shrimps 82

Spicy Sweet Potato Fries 36

Spinach And Mushroom Mini Quiche 26

Spinach Bacon Spread 18

Spinach Dip With Bread Knots 37

Sprouts Wraps Appetizer 27

Steak And Vegetable Skewers 74

Steak Kabobs With Vegetables 69

Steamed Pot Stickers 33

Stir-fried Chicken With Mixed Fruit 53

Stir-fried Steak And Cabbage 73

Strawberry Cheesecake Rolls 92

Stuffed Apples 101

Sumptuous Pizza Tortilla Rolls 74

Sweet And Spicy Pork Chops 75

Sweet Potatoes With Zucchini 43

Sweet-and-sour Polish Sausage 71

T

Tasty Pork Chops 73

Tasty Shrimp Bacon Wraps 33

Tender Salmon 90

Tex-mex Salmon Stir-fry 78

Tex-mex Turkey Burgers 64

Thyme Beef Roast 70

Tofu Bites 41

Tomato Pork Burgers 68

Tuna Veggie Stir-fry 79

Turkish Chicken Kebabs 53

Typical Cod Nuggets 89

U

Unstuffed Cabbage 76

V

Vanilla Chocolate Bites 99

Vanilla Cobbler With Hazelnut 97

Vanilla Cookies 101

Vanilla French Toast Sticks 15

Vanilla Muffins With Pecans 102

Vegetable Beef Meatballs With Herbs 72

Vegetable Pot Stickers 35

W

Warm Chicken And Spinach Salad 51

Whole Roasted Chicken 52

Y

Yellow Curry Chicken Thighs With Peanuts 55

Z

Zesty Garlic Scallops 79

Zoodles With Cheese 19

Zucchini And Potato Tots 34

Zucchini With Parmesan Cheese 36

Printed in Great Britain
by Amazon